Casting Nets wi

Endorsements

"Here is an irreplaceable guide for Catholics who want to become saints while making saints. I have known Chris Stewart and his work for many years. His passion for sharing the faith is contagious, and *Casting Nets with the Saints* will inspire many to do the same."

Chris Stefanick, best-selling author and president and founder of Real Life Catholic

"The Lord calls us to proclaim Jesus Christ, as missionary disciples of the New Evangelization. There are no better teachers than those who have gone before us, the communion of saints who have witnessed to the Gospel for two thousand years. *Casting Nets with the Saints* distills the lessons of the saints for the Catholics of today. This book is invaluable for anyone who wants to help the world encounter the love, mercy, and truth of Jesus Christ."

Bishop James Conley, Diocese of Lincoln

"*Casting Nets with the Saints* offers concrete and captivating examples of how to succeed in bringing the radiance of the Gospel to those most in need of its light. Chris Stewart weaves countless stories from the lives of the saints into a beautiful tapestry, showing how we can effectively win souls for God by following the examples of the greatest evangelists, the saints."

Jason Evert, author of Pure Faith *and* Saint John Paul the Great: His Five Loves

"Inspiration is all around us if we know where to look. This book inspires and invites all Christians to evangelize with support from the saints in heaven. It not only teaches effective evangelization but also introduces the reader to the lives of the saints who, though ordinary, loved and lived extraordinary lives. This book is a practical guide in how to be a saint and invite others as well!"

Leah Darrow, Catholic author and speaker

"One of the deepest needs in the Church today is that its members start evangelizing! Many just don't know how. Chris Stewart expertly and passionately shows, through the examples of the saints, how we too are called to share our faith. Read this book and be God's instrument of salvation!"

Fr. Larry Richards, president and founder of
The Reason for Our Hope Foundation

"An inspirational book! How could a book chock-full of the stories of some of the most exemplary men and women who ever lived not be? In a single volume, Chris Stewart makes the lives of so many canonized saints accessible, allowing them to reach out toward the hearts of his readers through his words. Pope Francis wrote, 'Missionary disciples accompany missionary disciples.' *Casting Nets with the Saints* is a link in this chain. A passionate and fervent missionary disciple himself, Chris Stewart opens up the lives of canonized missionary disciples, so that his readership of budding missionary disciples can benefit from their example of holiness and evangelization."

Steve Dawson, president and founder of
St. Paul Street Evangelization

"*Casting Nets with the Saints* is a definitive reference book depicting the lives of several saints—many well-known as well as some more obscure saints. Through the stories of their lives, we are given insights not only on how to evangelize but also on how to live our lives in a way that inspires others to become saints. I highly recommend this book to all—especially those who think they have to be superhuman or ultraholy before they can evangelize. Every Christian is called to evangelize, and this book is a great resource for all, especially those who may feel reluctant to do so. It would also be a wonderful gift for anyone who wants to know more about the saints and how to live a holier life."

Gail Buckley, president and founder of
Catholic Scripture Study International

"Want to become a better evangelist? Who better to learn from than those who fought the good fight and ended up in heaven? In his latest book, *Casting Nets with the Saints*, Chris Stewart offers advice on evangelization from those who know better than anyone. Don't try to reinvent the wheel. Tap into this great resource and get busy saving souls!"

Gary Zimak, speaker, author, and radio host,
FollowingTheTruth.com

"Fifty-six different saints … countless stories of inspiration. I couldn't put *Casting Nets with the Saints* down! If you are looking for new ways to grow in your faith and inspire others, look no further than the lives of the saints who paved the way before us. I am so thankful to Chris Stewart and Casting Nets for giving us this gem!"

Sarah Swafford, speaker and author of Emotional Virtue:
A Guide to Drama-Free Relationships

"If you want to be a saint, then do what they did. Chris Stewart's *Casting Nets with the Saints* shows you how."

Jon Leonetti, speaker and author of
Your God Is Too Boring

"Jesus's command to go into the world and spread the good news is as daunting today as it has always been. Nevertheless, the command and the call are not just for a chosen few. Christ's command to share the Gospel is part of the mission of all the baptized. In his latest book, *Casting Nets with the Saints*, Chris Stewart provides a practical manual for evangelization. Drawing deeply from the experience and example of the saints, Chris shows Catholics how to cast their nets and be true 'fishers of men.'"

Fr. Dwight Longenecker, blogger, author, and speaker

"What do the saints have to do with evangelization? Plenty! Author Chris Stewart underscores the expertise of the saints. No matter the century, saints communicate the Truth, which is the 'same yesterday and today and forever.' Stewart illustrates how the saints participate in our sanctification and shows us how they can become powerful 'missionary partners' with us. With 'souls on the line,' we can beseech evangelizing help from the saints so that none will be lost and heaven will rejoice. Highly recommended!"

Donna-Marie Cooper O'Boyle, EWTN host of several TV series, speaker, and award-winning author of more than twenty books, including The Kiss of Jesus *and* Feeding Your Family's Soul, *www.donnacooperoboyle.com*

"One of the first things Jesus said in Scripture was, 'Come and see.' In *Casting Nets with the Saints*, Chris Stewart invites us to a deeper understanding of Jesus's mission to reveal the Father and our role in bringing the good news to people around the world. Most importantly, Stewart calls us to embody Christ's final words to his followers to 'make disciples' in a hostile culture."

Patrick Novecosky, editor-in-chief of Legatus *magazine*

"Imagine if you could have someone research the lives of the saints for you and pull out the key details and stories that could inform and inspire your efforts in sharing the faith with others. That's exactly what Chris Stewart has done in *Casting Nets with the Saints*. A 'school' of sorts, from more than fifty saints' lives— inspiring stories, principles worth imitating, and insights to help us all be more effective in giving our faith away to others."

Jim Beckman, associate professor of leadership and discipleship at the Augustine Institute

Casting Nets

with the Saints

Learn from the Best
How to Share the Faith

CHRIS STEWART

With a foreword by **Deacon Harold Burke-Sivers**

**Our
Sunday
Visitor**

www.osv.com
Our Sunday Visitor Publishing Division
Our Sunday Visitor, Inc.
Huntington, Indiana 46750

About the Author

Chris Stewart is a gifted speaker whose talks on catechesis, theology, spirituality, and evangelization have moved audiences all over the United States for more than twenty years. He has a Master of Theological Studies from Ave Maria University and is cofounder of Casting Nets Ministries.

CONTENTS

Foreword

For far too long, we Catholics have been filled with a spirit of apathy and embarrassment about sharing our faith. We keep the faith to ourselves and contain it within the walls of the Church. When we are challenged by our friends and loved ones about why we are Catholic, we cower. When the culture tries to shove subjective truth down our throats, we worry about being politically correct. When unborn children are slaughtered and marriage is redefined, we remain silent or turn the other way. We must pray, of course, but we must also act and speak the Truth in love. We must go out with the Holy Spirit at our side, meet people where they are, and witness to them.

The saints are the quintessential examples of how to evangelize effectively, and through them Christ reveals who we are called to be. We cannot simply sit back and say, "I'm a good person" because there are no "good" people in heaven—only saints. The saints and their evangelizing witness form a foundation for holiness and make clear what is expected of a follower of Jesus. Their lives remind us that we are called to participate in the kingdom of heaven here on earth as evangelizing witnesses, influencing the culture with truth and love, compassion and mercy, peace and freedom—all qualities that flow from the very heart of God.

Casting Nets with the Saints is a spiritual nexus between effective evangelization and the lives of the saints. In this truly inspirational book, Chris Stewart leads us on a fascinating journey of encounter with fifty-six men and women who responded generously to the love of God showered on them. They have survived the pains and challenges of this world, they have washed their robes white in the blood of the Lamb, and now they rejoice and share in the total victory of Christ.

This extraordinary journey of learning to share the Gospel more effectively teaches us that in order to become saints, we don't need to be great theologians like St. Augustine or St. John Paul II. We don't need to be martyrs like St. Victor of Marseilles or Emil Kapaun. We don't need to be great leaders like St. Benedict and St. Elizabeth of Hungary. We don't even need to perform great works of charity like St. Teresa of Calcutta or St. Vincent de Paul. In order to become saints, we must allow ourselves to be totally consumed by the fire of God's absolute love. We become saints by fulfilling Christ's command to love the Lord our God with our whole heart, soul, mind, and strength, and then sharing the faith in love with everyone we meet.

To be saints means that we must seek union with the Father in love through the deepening and strengthening of our relationship with Jesus in the Holy Spirit. Jesus's call to sainthood begins with his command to us: "Be perfect, as your heavenly Father is perfect" (Mt 5:48). Holiness is a calling by God to share in his very life through desiring and striving for perfection in love. The way of holiness molds, shapes, and forms us into the Body of Christ—into Jesus himself. The more we act under God's Spirit, the more we seek to know and to do God's holy will in our lives. The more we implore the assistance and grace of the Holy Spirit, the more we grow in holiness and the closer we come to sainthood.

The saints presented in this book are as fascinating as they are diverse: men and women, adults and children, scholars and mystics, ancients and moderns. Many of these saints are household names (St. Patrick and St. Katharine Drexel), some are more obscure (St. Frances of Rome and St. Vitalis of

Gaza), and some I had never heard of (St. Hospitius and St. Clotilde). Yet they all share a common gift for sharing the faith with humility, mercy, and purity of heart. They were not afraid to stand up for and defend "the way, and the truth, and the life" (John 14:6), which is not an idea or philosophy, but the Person of Jesus Christ. They fought subjectivism, the idea that "truth is whatever I want it to be" that was rampant in their day, just as it is in ours. Like us, they lived in a world that believed that saints have no real value and that becoming a saint (i.e., living a holy and virtuous life) is a waste of time.

If we think of our world today as a vineyard, our culture tries to convince us that the rotting fruit it produces—which reeks of moral and spiritual decay—is actually good for us. The truth is, if we eat this fruit, we will become violently ill; and if we continue to eat it, we will inevitably die. This is why each and every one of us is called to be an evangelizing saint! We must share the good, life-giving fruit of the Gospel with people who are spiritually sick and dying.

The world is the field in which the word of God is sown. Through our efforts as evangelizing saints—as sowers of the seed of the Gospel of Jesus Christ—the world will bear rich fruit. Yet, like the saints in this book, we may not know what fruit we are producing, because it is God who picks and distributes the fruit of our labors. We may never know how someone was touched by something we said. We may never know how things turned out after someone came to us for advice. We may never know how someone's life was changed when they met Jesus in us. But as his saints, members of the Body of Christ making our way to heaven, we know that "God's love has been poured into our hearts by the Holy Spirit, and it is in this outpouring of love that the God who wishes to reveal Himself achieves his purpose and goals."[1]

You may be asking yourself, "But why am *I* called to evangelize? Isn't that the job of the clergy or for incredibly holy people like the saints?"

The answer is no, and that is precisely the point of *Casting Nets with the Saints*—by our baptism into Christ's death, we are called to be evangelizing disciples. A disciple is one who hears, accepts, and carries out the teaching of Jesus. A disciple follows and imitates Jesus. Each of us who has been baptized has this mission and calling: to share our experience of knowing Jesus Christ personally and to invite others to share in his life.

To be saints who do the work of evangelization, we must let God work in us. We must take our hands off the steering wheel and let God drive. We must empty ourselves of sin so that God can fill us with his love. We must die to the ways of this world so that Christ can live in us.

In this world of sin and darkness, Chris Stewart's *Casting Nets with the Saints* shows how poor and humble saints shine brightly. Through them, the light of Christ ignites our hearts and inspires us to respond lovingly to the Father's tender embrace. When we live out the mission of loving God and neighbor, we too become saints. We should rejoice and be glad, for our reward will be great in heaven.

DEACON HAROLD BURKE-SIVERS, M.T.S.
Author and EWTN series host
November 9, 2016

Introduction

Whether it is academics, business, or athletics, everyone wants to excel in his area of performance. We want to get better. Athletes or sports teams that desire to improve look to the best in their sport. Remember the Gatorade ad campaign of the 1990s, "Be Like Mike?" Many argue that Michael Jordan is the best basketball player to ever dribble a ball. So basketball players studied how he played, what he ate, and how he worked out, all with the hope of playing the game as well as he did. Startup businesses do not look to companies barely keeping the doors open but instead investigate successful Fortune 500 companies. If you are a student looking to improve your grades, you are not going to ask the "D" student to tutor you—you ask the valedictorian. If you picked up this book, then you want to improve your efforts as an evangelist. So where should we begin to look for help?

It is always exciting when friends, family, or people I encounter around the country ask me for advice on how to share the Gospel. Evangelization has become what I am passionate about, and that passion is matched only by my zeal to help others become the best evangelists they can become. Because of my theology degree, line of work, and love of the topic, people perceive me to be an expert on evangelization. But I must admit that my expertise has been gleaned not just from Scripture, the magisterium of the Church, the great popes of the New Evangelization, or learned theologians, but especially from the saints.

The saints remain *the* experts on evangelization. When studying the lives of the saints, it becomes evident that they were oases of conversions. The saints are who I look to for inspiration, guidance, and practical lessons for effectively communicating the Gospel. Pope Francis encourages us to do the same:

> It helps us to see that the Church's history is a history of salvation, to be mindful of those saints who inculturated the Gospel in the life of our peoples and to reap the fruits of the Church's rich bimillennial tradition, without pretending to come up with a system of thought detached from this treasury, as if we wanted to reinvent the Gospel. At the same time, this principle impels us to put the word into practice, to perform works of justice and charity which make that word fruitful. Not to put the word into practice, not to make it reality, is to build on sand, to remain in the realm of pure ideas and to end up in a lifeless and unfruitful self-centeredness.[2]

There is no need to reinvent the principles of evangelization when we have two thousand years of saints who have done it so well. Look to the road map that the saints have laid out for us to effectively engage our culture with the Gospel.

Some may be thinking, "Today's culture is so radically different from the past. How could learning how a saint shared the Gospel in the thirteenth century add to our efforts in the twenty-first century?" First let us hear how Pope Francis answers the same objection:

> We do well to keep in mind the early Christians and our many brothers and sisters throughout history who were filled with joy, unflagging courage and zeal in proclaiming the Gospel. Some people nowadays console themselves by saying that things are not as easy as they used to be, yet we know that the Roman Empire was not conducive to the Gospel message, the struggle for justice, or the defense of human dignity. Every period

of history is marked by the presence of human weakness, self-absorption, complacency and selfishness, to say nothing of the concupiscence which preys upon us all.... Let us not say, then, that things are harder today; they are simply different.[3]

Yes, every point in human history is different. However, human nature never changes. Ways of sinning may change, but sin and the remedy for it remain the same. The Eternal God who transforms the human heart never changes. Therefore, the saints, whether in the last century or the first century, were communicating the Truth that is the "same yesterday and today and for ever" (Heb 13:8).

Saints shine not just as teachers by example of evangelization but also as participants with us. Our brothers and sisters in heaven are presently interceding for us. They are cheering us on and praying for our salvation. If they are doing this for us, you can also be certain that they are praying for those we are trying to evangelize.

This book presents the wisdom of fifty-six saints and how they evangelized. I encourage you to do two things while you read it. First, think about which saints speak personally to you. Their background, circumstances or personality may remind you of yourself. Follow up with those saints you feel an attraction to. Study them and begin to form a relationship with them in your prayer life. Let those saints become your missionary partners. Let them become the Michael Jordan that you want to "Be Like" when it comes to evangelism.

Secondly, I am convinced that the saints in heaven play a major role in every conversion story. As you share the Gospel with someone, begin to pray for the saints and angels looking over this person to guide and assist your efforts. Many times while engaging a person with the Gospel, a particular saint jumps into my thoughts. Immediately I will begin to ask for that saint's intercession. I will study that saint's life to see what could be useful in sharing the Gospel with this particular person. It is amazing how different my evangelization is when this happens. But none of this will be possible if we continue to ignore our heavenly brothers and sisters who want to help our evangelization.

The fifty-six saints are divided into two parts of this book. The first part is *The Seven Pillars of Effective Evangelization*. Tony Brandt and I introduced The Seven Pillars in *Casting Nets: Grow Your Faith by Sharing Your Faith*.[4] These pillars comprise universal principles necessary for evangelization to produce fruit for any individual, parish, diocese, or institution. They are not steps to evangelization, nor do they constitute a program. Instead they are foundations that methods and programs can be built upon. In that first book we taught the principle of the pillar and then demonstrated it through personal stories from our combined forty-plus years of experience. In this book, the saints demonstrate the pillars.

In the second part of the book I focus on *The Seven Characteristics of an Effective Evangelist*. Like the pillars, these characteristics are both universal and necessary. These characteristics are manifested in individuals, but they also are evident in communities that are sharing the Gospel well. To become the best evangelists that we can be, we must work to acquire all seven of them. While the saints whom I cite illustrate one particular characteristic, you can rest assured that they possessed all of them — and that must be our aim as well.

The work of evangelization is too important not to do it well. Souls are on the line. Let us pray to all the holy men and women who have preceded us to intercede in our efforts of spreading the Gospel, so that the lost will be found, and there will be rejoicing in heaven today (cf. Lk 15:9–10).

Part One

The Saints and the
Seven Pillars
of Effective
Evangelization

ST. VINCENT FERRER

ST. GEMMA GALGANI

ST. ABRAHAM

ST. CATHERINE DE RICCI

Pillar 1

PRAYERFUL

Breathing is made up of two stages: inhaling, the intake of air, and exhaling, the letting out of this air. The spiritual life is fed, nourished, by prayer and is expressed outwardly through mission: inhaling—prayer—and then exhaling. When we inhale, by prayer, we receive the fresh air of the Holy Spirit. When exhaling this air, we announce Jesus Christ risen by the same Spirit. No one can live without breathing. It is the same for the Christian: without praise and mission there is no Christian life.

— Pope Francis [5]

When we think of the saints, we imagine them as spiritual giants. Some, like St. Vincent Ferrer, cast their nets far and wide and converted thousands. Some, like St. Boniface and St. Patrick, transformed entire nations from paganism to Catholicism. Others, like St. Thérèse of Lisieux, cast their nets and rescued thousands without setting foot out of their convents. Martyrs, like St. Stephen and St. Ignatius of Antioch, won souls in every land by freely giving up their lives for Christ. As saints cast their nets, they performed wonders. Some, like St. André Bessette, worked miracles; and some, like martyr St. Thomas More, forgave their persecutors.

But we must remember that the saints, even though they did extraordinary things, were ordinary women and men just like you and me. They were effective evangelizers because they grounded their lives on faithful prayer. They enjoyed a deeply prayerful relationship with Jesus produced by grace. Saints accomplished so much because they knew where the source of their strength lay: "I can do all things in him who strengthens me" (Phil 4:13). The axiom "you cannot give what you do not have" fits the saints well. They could give Christ to others because their lives overflowed with him (see Ps 23:5). For two thousand years, the prayer life of saints around the world has been the source of countless conversions. Therefore, if we are going to evangelize *well*, then our prayer life must become a *wellspring* overflowing with the life of Christ.

St. Vincent Ferrer (1350–1419) was a Spanish Dominican. Like many in the Order of Preachers, Vincent overflowed with a talent to communicate the Gospel. As a faithful son of St. Dominic, he did not take his natural gift for granted but prepared himself before every sermon with study and reflective prayer. Before one of his sermons Vincent received word that a prestigious nobleman would be in the congregation. Perhaps because of nerves or anxiety, Vincent spent all his valuable time studying to prepare for the sermon and left no time to pray. When the nobleman heard the sermon, he was unimpressed. By the grace of God, the nobleman came to hear Vincent again, but this time his presence was unknown to the saint. Vincent's preparation was his normal study *and* prayer. This time when the prestigious man of the world heard Vincent, he was profoundly moved. When Vincent was told of the two different responses to his preaching, he humbly and truthfully responded, "In the first sermon it was Vincent who preached. In the second sermon, it was Jesus Christ." You cannot give what you do not have.

The story of St. Monica praying for her morally lost son, Augustine, has brought hope to parents for many centuries. Monica's example demonstrates what prayer for conversion must look like—the prayer must have ***passion, purpose***, and ***perseverance***. For seventeen years Monica offered daily prayers to the Lord of Mercy with tears. As St. Ambrose told her, "It is impossible for the son of such tears to perish!" She focused singly on the conversion of her son. St. Augustine described the answer to his mother's prayers as the Lord "called, shouted and broke through my deafness." St. Monica could be the patroness of all prayers for the New Evangelization.

Passion must impel evangelistic prayers for conversion. The word "passion" comes from the Latin *passio*, which means "to suffer." If you have family and friends not practicing the faith, which is probably everyone reading this book, have you felt pain and suffering and even cried over their loss of faith? If the answer is "yes," then let me share some good news … it is precisely in that pain and suffering that we are nearest to the heart of our Savior. As much as you long for them to come to Christ, you can be assured that he wants it even more. As Jesus said to St. Faustina, "The loss of each soul plunges Me into mortal sadness. You always console Me when you pray for sinners. The prayer most pleasing to Me is prayer for the conversion of sinners."[6] So do not shy away from that pain or those tears; instead, let them make your prayers even more passionate.

A fourth-century Egyptian monk and disciple of St. Pachomius named ***St. Abraham***[7] (d. 372) was a man whose prayers were full of passion. After the death of his brother, Abraham was put in charge of the care of his niece Mary. With diligence Abraham raised Mary in the faith, but after twenty years her faith lapsed. Mary left Abraham and plunged into a life of sin. (It is amazing how all too familiar this story seems to be today.) For two years straight, Abraham prayed and cried for his niece. His sorrow was turned to joy when he found Mary, and they had a passionate conversation that led to her repentance. Mary returned with her uncle with the grace of not only forgiveness but also the ability to work miracles. She is now recognized as a saint. Let your passion fill your prayers for the lost.

Evangelistic prayers must have a real *purpose*. These are not prayers for health or material needs (of course we should pray for these intentions as well), but for the salvation of souls. They are passionate prayers offered for the grace of conversion. This might seem to be a no-brainer, but we must refocus our attention on what is truly important in our works of evangelization. While on earth Jesus did works of mercy, worked miracles, and taught often, but what was his mission? Jesus came to establish the kingdom of heaven. He came for the salvation of souls. If we are his disciples, then his purpose is our purpose. Our prayers should reflect this mission as well. Jesus told St. Faustina, "Call upon My mercy on behalf of sinners; I desire their salvation. When you say this prayer, with a contrite heart and with faith on behalf of some sinner, I will give him the grace of conversion. This is the prayer: 'O Blood and Water, which gushed forth from the Heart of Jesus as a fount of Mercy for us, I trust in You.'"[8] Do not let a prayer time end without offering up this purpose.

The young, beautiful Italian **St. Gemma Galgani** (1878–1903) understood the purpose of praying for conversions. Fr. Germanus Ruoppolo was with Gemma during one of her mystical encounters with the Lord. Gemma begged for the salvation of a stranger she had met in her home town. The Lord informed her that this soul was lost, and justice would be required for his sins. The young saint would not take no for an answer and continued to plead, "You have shed Thy Blood for him as well as for me. Will You save me and not him? I will not rise from here. Save him. Promise me that You will save him." This exchange went back and forth with neither side giving in. Finally, Gemma won the Lord's heart when she invoked the intercession of his Blessed Mother. Fr. Germanus heard Gemma cry out, "He is saved, he is saved! You hast conquered, Jesus." Soon after there was a knock at the door requesting Father to hear a confession. The astonished priest reported, "I thought my heart would burst. It was Gemma's sinner, converted that hour." Our prayers for the lost will be filled with hope if they are strengthened with *perseverance*. As with most things in life, we do not achieve our desired ends with brief efforts; instead, success typically follows long-endured efforts. When we sincerely pray for the salvation of souls, we will face distractions, struggles, despair, and temptations to quit. The Apostle of Divine Mercy, St. Faustina shared a temptation she faced when Satan told her, "'Do not pray for sinners, but for yourself, for you will be damned.' Paying no attention to Satan, I continued to pray with redoubled fervor for sinners. The Evil Spirit howled with fury, 'Oh, if I had power over you!' and disappeared."[9] Do not give in! Push through, persevere with your daily prayers for souls are on the line!

An Italian Dominican nun, **St. Catherine de Ricci** (1522–1589) taught about persistent prayer by word and example. A well-known despicable criminal who had been sentenced to death was brought to the attention of Catherine. The thief had fallen into despair, was angry and hateful. He was closed off to any attempts to reconcile him to the Divine Judge before he met him face-to-face. The saint pleaded for the salvation of the criminal's soul. She offered her prayers and to take on herself whatever inflictions were justly due for his sins. The sinner was so thoroughly changed that he went to confession in tears, was peaceful with his punishment, and even preached to the assembled crowd at his execution that they should flee from their own sins. St. Catherine taught, "We must bring to prayer a great confidence that we shall be heard.... When we desire to obtain a favor from Almighty God, we must go on asking for it until we get it; because He has determined the number of times we are to ask for it; and He will not grant our petition till that number is complete." We must be like the persistent widow (cf Lk 18:1–8) with our noble supplication for souls. For the price of salvation might be our perseverance.

If our prayers for the grace of conversion for family, friends, coworkers, and even strangers have passion, purpose, and perseverance, then we can bring them to repentance. Pray for a heart like the Divine Redeemer, a heart for the lost. Have confidence that the Lord hears your prayers. Our Lord told St. Faustina, "By your entreaties, obtain for them trust in My mercy, because they have most need of trust, and have it the least. Be assured that the grace of eternal salvation for certain souls in their final moment depends on your prayer."[10] What a noble task the Lord has entrusted to us! Our prayers are the essential part of a soul's invitation to come to Christ.

ST. VINCENT DE PAUL

ST. CATHERINE OF SIENA

ST. NORBERT

ST. PATRICK

Pillar 2

INVITATIONAL

We cannot forget that evangelization is first and foremost about preaching the Gospel to *those who do not know Jesus Christ or who have always rejected him.* Many of them are quietly seeking God, led by a yearning to see his face, even in countries of ancient Christian tradition. All of them have a right to receive the Gospel. Christians have the duty to proclaim the Gospel without excluding anyone. Instead of seeming to impose new obligations, they should appear as people who wish to share their joy, who point to a horizon of beauty and who invite others to a delicious banquet. It is not by proselytizing that the Church grows, but "by attraction."

— Pope Francis [11]

How many weddings do you show up to without being invited? Or how many business meetings do you attend without receiving an invitation? Whether we greatly desire to attend an event or would like to find any excuse to avoid an event, the fact of the matter is, our attendance will never happen without an invitation. The good news of salvation still remains the best news in human history, but if we do not invite others to receive the Gospel, then it becomes nothing more than a historical event. Throughout history saints function as the instruments of invitation; through their words and actions, through their life and death, they sought to invite others to a relationship with Jesus Christ in his holy Church.

Long before our beloved St. Teresa dressed the wounds of the dying in the ghettos of Calcutta, the seventeenth century gave birth to her predecessor, **St. Vincent de Paul** (1581–1660). He spent his life comforting the poor and calling the rich to do likewise; hence today there are St. Vincent de Paul Societies around the world continuing that unceasing work. However, most do not know of Vincent's time as a slave. As he sailed on the Mediterranean Sea to Narbonne for a trip, three African vessels overtook Vincent's ship. A series of men enslaved him, and Vincent eventually became the property of a Muslim chemist who took a liking to him. The chemist encouraged Vincent to give up Christianity for Islam, upon which he would be the heir to all his property and to freedom. Vincent refused. As time wore on, he became the property of the chemist's nephew, who was raised a Christian but had converted to Islam.

One of the wives of the master took an interest in Vincent because of his joy and demeanor while at work. After many conversations, Vincent and his faith fascinated and piqued her interest. She shared a simple invitation with her husband:

> I have been talking to your white slave that works in the garden about his religion—the religion which was once yours. It seems full of good things and so is he. You need never watch him as you do the other men, and the overseer has not had to beat him once. Why, then, did you give up that religion for another? In that, my lord, you did not do well.[12]

His eyes were opened to the Truth, but to leave Islam could result in his own peril. He and Vincent disguised themselves and fled to France. After two years of captivity, Vincent de Paul grew to become the saint we know of today. His former master converted back to Christianity and entered a monastery—all because of a simple invitation to return to the faith of his birth.

Do not be afraid to invite someone back to the faith! An invitation is not forcing your faith on someone; it remains simply an invitation. Like holiness, faith cannot be imposed on someone, but only proposed. This is how our gentle Lord works with us. "He always invites us to take a step forward," says Pope Francis, "but does not demand a full response if we are not yet ready. He simply asks that we sincerely look at our life and present ourselves honestly before him, and that we be willing to continue to grow, asking from him what we ourselves cannot as yet achieve."[13] When you invite someone to an event, you do not "force" that event on them. Your invitation offers a modest request to partake of a journey, a journey on which we are willing to walk with them, beside them, as Pope Francis describes:

> One who accompanies others has to realize that each person's situation before God and their life in grace are mysteries which no one can fully know from without. The Gospel tells us to correct others and to help them to grow on the basis of a recognition of the objective evil of their actions (cf. Mt 18:15), but without making judgments about their responsibility and culpability (cf. Mt 7:1; Lk 6:37). Someone good at such accompaniment does not give in to frustrations or fears. He or she invites others to let themselves be healed, to take up their mat, embrace the cross, leave all behind and go forth ever anew to proclaim the Gospel. Our personal experience of being accompanied and assisted, and of

openness to those who accompany us, will teach us to be patient and compassionate with others, and to find the right way to gain their trust, their openness and their readiness to grow.[14]

Yet, our humble invitations might change all of eternity for those we encounter.

There exists little debate that *St. Catherine of Siena* (1347–1380) is one of the strongest and most influential women the Church has ever known. While Catherine lived a short life, the lives she touched and perhaps the history of the Church were changed forever. Her influence on her family and friends was extraordinary. A friend of Catherine introduced her to a worldly gentleman, Francesco Malavolti. Francesco, hardened of heart and certain that this woman would not have the same effect on him as she did on his weak-minded friend, found himself in awe of the saint. After the encounter he repented, went to confession, changed his life, and became a devout friend of Catherine. When friends of Francesco harassed him about his newfound "boring" life, he encouraged them to meet Catherine, just once. Amazingly, they too experienced the loving God. What a great example of what I call "third-party evangelization!" Maybe your family and friends do not want to hear the Gospel from you, but there may be a faithful friend whom you can invite them to meet. Is there a book, movie, audio talk, or article you can invite them to experience? Or has someone written an article on social media networks that you can share with them? It is amazing how when someone else is saying it (even though it could be exactly what we have always said), our loved ones seem more open to the Truth conveyed.

Perhaps the most well-known story of Catherine of Siena is her influence over Pope Gregory XI. At that time, popes lived in Avignon, France, instead of Rome, a period known as the Avignon Papacy (1309–1377). Catherine, feeling a commission from God, traveled to Avignon to convince Pope Gregory to return to Rome. For three months Catherine persisted with an unwavering strength, inviting the Supreme Pontiff to go back to his chair in Rome. After resisting for three months, Gregory finally relinquished the fight and promised the young woman that he would head to Rome. Shortly after Catherine returned home to Siena, she heard reports that the pope was having cold feet, being influenced by the French cardinals. Catherine dictated letters to Gregory imploring him to keep his promise, to be bold and have no fear. Thanks to Catherine's letters, persistence, and especially her prayers, Pope Gregory XI returned to Rome on January 17, 1377. Our invitations to the Gospel must be persistent. Has someone said no to your invitation to a church event? Ask again! If St. Catherine went home after the first time the pope said no, then Church history might look dramatically different. What will eternity look like if you do not gently invite again?

St. Norbert (1080–1134), archbishop of Magdeburg, Germany, and founder of the Premonstratensians (which became known as the Norbertines), greatly reformed the clergy and laity during his life. Theobald, Count of Champagne, already a deeply religious man, desired to join Norbert in his order's way of life. The saint must have been overjoyed to have a prospective follower so young, passionate, and faithful (and yes, influential). Adding Theobald to Norbert's religious order would surely get the attention of the nobility and benefit his work greatly. However, Norbert took Theobald's request to prayer.

After several days of prayer and discernment, Norbert shared with the young noble his decision. Norbert told Theobald, "You will not be a religious, you will continue to bear the yoke of the Lord as you have done, and you will add to it that of wedlock." Norbert then gave the young man a white scapular to wear under his clothes and a rule of life that would lead to holiness and could be accomplished outside of a monastery. This would be the first known case of a laity living in the world and yet affiliated with a religious order. Who knows what Norbert heard or felt in his prayer about Theobald, but whatever it was, it lead to a personal invitation fit for Theobald. We must constantly discern WHAT it is we are inviting people to. Not all are ready for a weekend retreat or a Bible study. Some are ready to ask questions about vocation or to think about going to Mass again for the first time in decades. It is our duty to discern what it is we will invite our family, friends, coworkers, and strangers to so that they can be open to what the Spirit has prepared for them.

If a top-ten list existed of the best evangelists of the two thousand years of Church history, ***St. Patrick*** (387–461) must certainly be considered. He is credited with the conversion of an entire country that in turn became missionaries to the entire world. The impact of this Irish priest on the Church in the United States cannot be underestimated. When Patrick set about his task of bringing the Gospel to the Emerald Isle, he had a laser-like focus on one group of people: the kings. He spent the majority of his missionary time attempting to convert the roughly one hundred kings of Ireland at the time. Patrick believed that if he could convince the kings of Christianity, then their subjects would follow. His theory proved to bear much fruit.

Obviously, Patrick believed the Gospel of Jesus Christ exists for everyone, even those not in power. However, his method to reach everyone involved targeting people with the most influence. Over twenty years of ministry, I have come to the same conclusion. If we try to bring people of influence to

Christ, they are going to bring others with them. Whether in our parishes, youth groups, schools, workplaces, or families, ask: Who is the most influential person in this community? Whom do people follow, not necessarily because they are in a leadership role but because they possess that charism of leadership? Have we invited them to a full life in Christ? Can you imagine how many souls could come to know the loving mercy of our Lord if this person became a powerful light of the Hope of Salvation? All of this is possible with the mighty stroke of an invitation.

Today's secular culture gives us great fear when extending invitations. We fear being called intolerant or a radical. Many times we presume the answer to our invitation will be no; therefore, we do not ask. But we do not know the answer! It is our responsibility to invite and allow the Holy Spirit to do what he does best: move hearts. If we have discerned what we are inviting people to, then we should have no fear. Whether it is a leader in the community or you need to bring in a faithful friend, have confidence that the Lord of all hearts desires what you desire: their salvation.

Pillar 3

HOSPITABLE

Being Church means being God's people, in accordance with the great plan of his fatherly love. This means that we are to be God's leaven in the midst of humanity. It means proclaiming and bringing God's salvation into our world, which often goes astray and needs to be encouraged, given hope and strengthened on the way. The Church must be a place of mercy freely given, where everyone can feel welcomed, loved, forgiven and encouraged to live the good life of the Gospel.

— Pope Francis [15]

An invitation means nothing if, when a person attends an event, retreat, parish, or home, he or she is not made to feel welcomed. When guests arrive in our churches and communities, it is imperative that they feel this is where they belong, that this is family, and this is what they long for. However, our sense of being hospitable must move beyond our natural capabilities. Our welcome must indeed be so real that it gives people a taste of their eternal home. Have you ever spent time with someone you believed was a living saint? Do you remember the feeling of wanting to linger in their presence and longing for the next time you would see them? The saints are sanctuaries of the Lord's loving arms.

A Doctor of the Church, ***St. Francis de Sales*** (1567–1622) lived in the wake of the Protestant Reformation. His book *Introduction to the Devout Life* has become one of the top spiritual classics of the last five hundred years. When Francis became bishop of Geneva, his zeal for bringing lost souls home to the Church embodied the Father's welcoming arms to the world. At the time Geneva was a Calvinist stronghold, and yet Francis would speak to them with the same tenderness as he would to his own flock: "Come, my dear children, come, let me put my arms around you. Ah, let me hide you in the bottom of my heart! God and I will help you." This compassion led to the conversion of seventy-two thousand Calvinists.

The saint's compassion for sinners and heretics scandalized his contemporaries. Francis answered his critics, "I would rather account to God for too great gentleness than for too great severity. Is not God all love?" Is our depth of compassion to the lost, the marginalized, enemies, or sinners scandalous? This is the degree to which Christ showed his love and for which the saints who follow him strive. Francis said, "You will catch more flies with a spoonful of honey than with a hundred barrels of vinegar. Were there anything better or fairer on earth than gentleness, Jesus Christ would have taught it us; and yet He has given us only two lessons to learn of Him—meekness and humility of heart."

But I can already hear complaints: "We must stand against sinful behavior." True, we must combat sin in all its forms, that being first and foremost the sin within ourselves. One of the major complaints against Jesus was that he ate with "sinners." The call of compassion is clear. It is not our responsibility to judge a person; and while we can never condone a sin, we must never condemn a person. A great Dominican theologian said, "The Church is intolerant in principle because she believes; she is tolerant in practice because she loves. The enemies of the Church are tolerant in principle because they do not believe; they are intolerant in practice because they do not love."[16] Only our welcoming gentleness will be a light to bring the lost home.

A fascinating queen of the thirteenth century, **St. Elizabeth of Hungary** (1207–1231) epitomized the gift of hospitality. Her generosity to the poor grew so extravagant that those in the court complained to her husband, King Louis IV of Thuringia. The king, being a pious man himself, questioned her accuser to see whether the queen's behavior had done damage to the kingdom, but the answer was obviously no. Therefore, he defended his wife: "As for her charities, they will bring upon us the divine blessings. We shall not want so long as we let her relieve the poor as she does." Elizabeth's care for the poor proved to be compassion for people and their dignity as human beings. Prudence characterized her charity, as she would find jobs or hire those who had the ability.

Elizabeth desired to bring the sick into her very house, and many times she welcomed them to her door. However, the castle of Wartburg sat upon a steep hill. The climb up to the castle created so much difficulty it was called "the knee smasher." Our saintly queen of generosity built a hospital at the bottom of the hill to overcome this obstacle. While I am sure that the poor were overjoyed at being able to have their needs met without climbing an unforgiving rock, I cannot help but be inspired by the beauty of this image and its application to evangelization. In our sin and brokenness, we would never have been able to reach God, so he lowered himself to us (cf. Phil 2:6–11). God came down the mountain to heal our wounds and feed our hunger, which is exactly what Elizabeth did. In our work of evangelization, we must also strive to meet the needs of those spiritually broken and hungry. Pope Francis has been trying to push us out the door to the bottom of the mountain:

The Church which "goes forth" is a community of missionary disciples who take the first step, who are involved and supportive, who bear fruit and rejoice. An evangelizing community knows that the Lord has taken the initiative, he has loved us first (cf. 1 Jn 4:19), and therefore we can move forward, boldly take the initiative, go out to others, seek those who have fallen away, stand at the crossroads and welcome the outcast. Such a community has an endless desire to show mercy, the fruit of its own experience of the power of the Father's infinite mercy. Let us try a little harder to take the first step and to become involved.[17]

We cannot simply wait in our castles (parishes, schools, and homes) for those needing the Savior to come to us; we must go to them.

The young virgin and martyr *St. Dorothy* (d. ca. 311) is buried at an ancient church in Rome named after her. She died under the Emperor Diocletian for refusing to worship the Roman pagan gods. On the way to her saintly death, a lawyer named Theophilus ridiculed her with a mocking tongue by asking her to send him some fruit from the "garden" to which she was proceeding (this "heavenly paradise" worth dying for). Moments before Dorothy's execution, she prayed for her enemies and that lawyer. An angel appeared with three roses and three apples for Theophilus. When he tasted the fruit, he converted to Christianity and eventually faced the same end as Dorothy. Both are included in the *Roman Martyrology*.

I have heard a few people express attitudes of, "why waste time with making our churches welcoming, developing hospitality teams or committees, when it is the sacraments and grace that save souls?" I agree one hundred percent: It is

Jesus Christ, through his grace and the sacraments, who saves souls. However, it is the desire of the Divine Messiah to use each of us to bring others to encounter that grace in the sacraments. The Lord, through his grace, transforms our small acts of hospitality into the supernatural efforts of encounter. If receiving an apple can change a fourth-century lawyer's life, then the fruits of our welcome at a Christmas Mass to someone who has not stepped foot in a church in more than five years can as well. Perhaps inviting a neighbor over for a casual dinner or offering a sincere "How is your day going?" to a coworker becomes the very act that God transforms into a supernatural event, allowing his light and love to radically change their lives.

A religious order proven to have had one of the biggest impacts on the Church is the one founded by **St. Benedict of Nursia** (480–547). The Benedictines constitute the world's largest monastic order, and their influence cannot be denied when the order can boast of having given the Church 200 cardinals, 7,000 archbishops, 15,000 bishops, and 1,560 canonized saints throughout its history. The Church's worship in Mass, Liturgy of the Hours, prayer life, and theology owe a great deal to the Benedictines. However, an often-overlooked virtue of the Benedictines is their spirit of hospitality. Hospitality became a virtue taught by the founder himself, and to this day Benedictine monasteries will have a guesthouse with a guest master monk ready to serve the pilgrim as if he or she were Christ. Benedict devoted a small chapter in the Rule to the spirit of being hospitable:

> Let all guests who arrive be received like Christ, for He is going to say, "I came as a guest, and you received Me" (Mt. 25:35). And to all let due honor be shown, especially to the domestics of the faith and to pilgrims.

As soon as a guest is announced, therefore, let the Superior or the brethren meet him with all charitable service. And first of all let them pray together, and then exchange the kiss of peace....

After the guests have been received and taken to prayer, let the Superior or someone appointed by him sit with them. Let the divine law be read before the guest for his edification, and then let all kindness be shown him....

Let the Abbot give the guests water for their hands; and let both Abbot and community wash the feet of all guests. After the washing of the feet let them say this verse: "We have received Your mercy, O God, in the midst of Your temple" (Ps.47[48]:10).

In the reception of the poor and of pilgrims the greatest care and solicitude should be shown, because it is especially in them that Christ is received; for as far as the rich are concerned, the very fear which they inspire wins respect for them.[18]

For a millennium and a half, Benedictine hospitality has opened hearts to the life-changing experience that is Jesus Christ.

The miracles that surround Benedict during his life are as inspiring as they are numerous. The saint read souls, prophesied the future, cast out demons, and raised people from the dead; and as if that were not enough, he could also move rocks! As the monks were building the cells of the monastery, they needed to remove a huge boulder. Three monks attempted to separate the boulder from the earth but failed. More monks were called in for reinforcements, and yet the boulder would not budge. The monks perceived that perhaps there was a supernatural force making removal impossible.

So the monks called in "special forces"; Benedict prayed and blessed their efforts. The monks immediately removed the boulder as if it were air. This simple story of the saint of hospitality offers up a beautiful analogy for the work of evangelization. Normally, when someone is not in relationship with Christ and his Church it is because of some "boulder" in his or her life: a past hurt, a preconceived idea of Christians, a lack of knowledge. A person's boulder could be big or small. As Pope Francis points out, we Christians might be the reason for their boulder.

> We must recognize that if part of our baptized people lack a sense of belonging to the Church, this is also due to certain structures and the occasionally unwelcoming atmosphere of some of our parishes and communities, or to a bureaucratic way of dealing with problems, be they simple or complex, in the lives of our people. In many places an administrative approach prevails over a pastoral approach, as does a concentration on administering the sacraments apart from other forms of evangelization.[19]

Removing these "boulders" or obstacles is many times what opens up a person to the idea of faith. Of course prayer, as mentioned in Chapter 1, plays a crucial role in this, but being authentically hospitable is our natural way to make boulders fly away like air to allow the Light of Christ to shine.

Invitations come in a variety of ways. They can be far and wide, personal and persistent, in our bulletins or on billboards. But the fact remains, all of our invitations will mean nothing if, when people come, they are not shown a deep, abiding hospitality. Even small welcoming acts, if done with a great intention, can produce unimaginable fruit. Jesus spoke of such acts done for his disciples: "Whoever gives to one of these little ones even a cup of cold water because he is a disciple, truly, I say to you, he shall not lose his reward" (Mt 10:42). If it remains true for his disciples, how much more does it apply to the lost souls whom Jesus, the Good Shepherd, cared for so much? Our hospitality, if sincere, authentic, and filled with joy, will be exactly what opens up the person to a truly inspiring, life-changing message.

Pillar 4

INSPIRATIONAL

Above all the Gospel must be proclaimed by witness. Take a Christian or a handful of Christians who, in the midst of their own community, show their capacity for understanding and acceptance, their sharing of life and destiny with other people, their solidarity with the efforts of all for whatever is noble and good. Let us suppose that, in addition, they radiate in an altogether simple and unaffected way their faith in values that go beyond current values, and their hope in something that is not seen and that one would not dare to imagine. Through this wordless witness these Christians stir up irresistible questions in the hearts of those who see how they live: Why are they like this? Why do they live in this way? What or who is it that inspires them?

— Pope Paul VI [20]

I still remember the day my firstborn daughter entered the world. This day changed my life forever, and since then every day is now lived differently because of that event. Similarly, two thousand years ago an event occurred that not only changed my life but defined the reality of what it means for me to "live." Jesus Christ suffered and died on a cross to pay the debt for our sin and walked out of a tomb to restore our life. This is good news! The resurrection power of Jesus Christ enables us to live differently every day and still changes lives around us. It has the power to bring the dead to life, transform despair to hope, and bring sadness to joy—TODAY! Do you believe this? This Gospel not only inspired the saints, but it also filled the saints with such a zeal that they spoke and lived it in a way that others were also inspired to a new life in Christ.

In the historically rich land of Italy, the place of martyrs, catacombs, and popes, only one owns the title of "Apostle of Italy." ***St. Bernardine of Siena*** (1380–1444) was born just about two hundred years after his spiritual father, St. Francis of Assisi. By the time of Bernardine's death, the Franciscans would experience one of their greatest renewals, especially in returning to the strict observance of the rule of St. Francis. Bernardine was zealous for souls, and that zeal was only matched by his talent to preach the Truth of the Gospel. Wherever he preached, hearts were touched and lives were renewed in Christ. When asked how one could preach with such fruit, Bernardine answered, "In all your actions seek in the first place the kingdom of God and his glory; direct all you do purely to his honor; persevere in brotherly charity, and practice first all that you desire to teach others. By this means the Holy Ghost will be your master, and will give you such wisdom and such a tongue that no adversary will be able to stand against you." The closer the messenger can get to the *Message,* the more effective each will be in reaching the desired end. This fundamental principle has not changed since St. Bernardine walked the highways of Italy, and in fact is crucial to the work of the New Evangelization, as Pope Francis teaches:

Whoever wants to preach must be the first to let the word of God move him deeply and become incarnate in his daily life.... Before preparing what we will actually say when preaching, we need to let ourselves be penetrated by that word which will also penetrate others, for it is a living and active word, like a sword "which pierces to the division of soul and spirit, of joints and marrow, and discerns the thoughts and intentions of the heart" (Heb 4:12). This has great pastoral importance. Today too, people prefer to listen to witnesses: they "thirst for authenticity" and "call for evangelizers to speak of a God whom they themselves know and are familiar with, as if they were seeing him."[21]

Why were the saints so successful in bringing lost sheep back to the Good Shepherd? Through them, his voice could be heard.

Once in the city of Bologna, Bernardine preached against the vices that plagued the local community. At this time many people were given to an addiction to gambling. The passionate preaching of the saint so moved these individuals that they quickly repented. Bernardine encouraged the penitents to make a sacrificial offering of their past vices with a bonfire in the public square, burning their playing cards, dice, and other devices of gambling. As any business owner could imagine, the local producer of playing cards was enraged with Bernardine. Our wise saint encouraged the entrepreneur to turn his attention to making cards with the Holy Name of Jesus on them. The business owner could hardly keep the cards in stock as he made more profit than ever before. In today's culture, there are many addicting distractions that consume our time, and they find their way into our lives by insidious methods. Like gambling, not all distractions are intrinsically evil (some are by nature evil); but TV, social media, hobbies, smartphones, and sports are so attractively entertaining that it is difficult—and at times seems impossible—to get people's attention with the faith. Bernardine of Siena taught us that if our lives authentically match up to the Gospel, then inspirational words not only compete but win the day against today's distractions.

If you are like me and have experienced failures in your efforts of evangelization, then Winfrid, the Archbishop of Mainz, better known as **St. Boniface** (ca. 675–754) is the saint for you. The "Apostle of Germany" had great success in bringing unbelievers to belief, but only after a failed missionary trip. The first mission trip was so poor that Boniface made the decision to return to Germany only if he had a direct commission from the Holy Father. With such a mandate, Winfrid became "Boniface," and Germany became Christian.

A potent image exists in the story of Boniface and the sacred oak tree dedicated to Thor. The local people clung to their exceedingly superstitious beliefs about their pagan gods. Instead of beating around the bush, Boniface decided to beat the tree directly. The people steadfastly believed that this tree belonged to Thor and he would protect it. With ax in hand, the saint chopped down the oak tree, and with almost one blow the tree splintered into four parts. Waiting for Thor to take his revenge proved a fruitless suspense. After nothing happened, the people realized their gods were defenseless against this Christ God whom Boniface embodied. St. Boniface used the lumber to build a church, and the rest is history. (For many Catholics with German heritage, it is a very important history.) The beauty of this story is that once shown the futile nature of sin, any sinner can be inspired to seek the life that will never fail nor disappoint. When inspirational lives show joy, passion, and love, it cuts through the emptiness of sin for those who are witnesses to such a life.

History credits an Augustinian monk, *St. Nicholas of Tolentine* (1245–1305), with raising more than one hundred children from the dead. He also was successful in raising hearts back to the spiritual life. During the saint's life, Tolentine was entangled in civil war, sinfulness, schism, and strife between political rulers and the Holy Father. (Sounds familiar.) Modest, quiet witness of the faith would not be enough during this time. As an evangelist, I often hear the words accredited to St. Francis of Assisi, "Preach the Gospel always, and only use words when necessary." There are times when words are necessary; at least Nicholas believed so. Another saint said of Nicholas's words, "He spoke of the things of heaven. Sweetly he preached the divine word, and the words that came from his lips fell like burning flame." Words can be effective inspiration.

As for any effective evangelist, there was opposition. During Nicholas's preaching, one such bully would shout and make a commotion. The intimidator would even begin fencing with his friends to scatter and distract the audience. Nicholas refused to be intimidated, however, and continued to proclaim the Truth with inspired words. Eventually the activist put his sword in its sheath and began to listen to the two-edged sword of the Gospel (cf. Heb 4:12). He was cut to the heart; he asked for forgiveness from Nicholas and began to live a new life. In today's world, a world that allows us to live in our own personal bubbles, words are necessary. Thanks to self-checkout lanes, for example, we do not even have to speak to a person when grocery shopping. Words, when marked with the clarity and charity of the Holy Spirit, can inspire the hardened heart to beat again.

The Holy Martyrs of the Church serve as an indispensable sign of inspiration from the first century to the present day. One such martyr is *St. Victor of Marseilles* (d. ca. 290), who received his ultimate heavenly reward under the persecution of Emperor Maximian. When the new emperor began his reign in Gaul, the first thing Victor did was visit the growing Christian flock. From house to house he visited, inspiring and encouraging them to rest in the fact that earthly death is but the beginning to eternal beatitude. When the emperor received word of what an officer of the Roman army was undertaking, he immediately arrested Victor. Bound and dragged through the streets of Gaul, Victor still refused to offer worship to a false god. He remained resolute in spite of being placed on the rack and stretched. Still not giving in, he was thrown into a dark, forlorn dungeon. Here Victor would become a light in the darkness and a water source for the thirsty.

While in the dungeon Victor prayed for the strength and consolation of the Lord. A brilliant light appeared about him, and angels could be heard singing. Struck to the heart, the guards in charge of Victor's confinement begged the saint for forgiveness and craved the waters of baptism. Victor urged them to seek out a priest, and then left his confinement with the guards and a priest for the seashore. Once baptized, the guards and Victor promptly returned to his dungeon. Maximian was beside himself with anger when he received the news of the conversion of the guards. Immediately the emperor arrested them and gave them the opportunity to renounce Christ or suffer losing their heads. So inspired and true was their conversion that all three persevered to the crown of martyrdom. Soon after Victor would suffer more torture, mutilation, and finally suffer the same fate as his new converts. When a Christian faces suffering, tribulations, and the prospect of death, it is in these moments that we are given opportunities to shine in the darkness and give drink to the thirsty in the middle of our cultural desert, as Pope Francis described:

"In the desert we rediscover the value of what is essential for living; thus in today's world there are innumerable signs, often expressed implicitly or negatively, of the thirst for God, for the ultimate meaning of life. And in the desert people of faith are needed who, by the example of their own lives, point out the way to the Promised Land and keep hope alive." In these situations we are called to be living sources of water from which others can drink.[22]

Our belief in eternal life must inspire us to suffer in a way that is entirely beyond this life and thereby inspire others to look for something more, something worth living a new life for.

The Gospel message still has the power to change lives today. With our bold witness, both in action and in word, we can proclaim the Truth that there is more to life. We can display the Truth that sin will never satisfy our deepest desires. Jesus Christ defeated sin and death two thousand years ago by his suffering, death, and resurrection. That same resurrection power can heal our suffering and brokenness today. This message is one we must shout to the hilltops, for this is what people are longing for even if they do not know they are in need of the Lord's mercy. The authentic message of the Gospel becomes the impulse that will inspire true conversion and give someone a desire to meet Christ in a tangible manner.

Pillar 5

SACRAMENTAL

Evangelization thus exercises its full capacity when it achieves the most intimate relationship, or better still, a permanent and unbroken intercommunication, between the Word and the sacraments. In a certain sense it is a mistake to make a contrast between evangelization and sacramentalization, as is sometimes done. It is indeed true that a certain way of administering the sacraments, without the solid support of catechesis regarding these same sacraments and a global catechesis, could end up by depriving them of their effectiveness to a great extent. The role of evangelization is precisely to educate people in the faith in such a way as to lead each individual Christian to live the sacraments as true sacraments of faith—and not to receive them passively or reluctantly.

— Pope Paul VI [23]

Everything that Jesus Christ did, from his Incarnation to his preaching, death, resurrection, and ascension, was to accomplish one goal: humanity's reconciliation with God. Jesus is the one true Savior of the World; he is "the way, and the truth, and the life" (Jn 14:6). The first four pillars of effective evangelization have one purpose: to bring someone to an authentic, abiding relationship with Jesus Christ in order that they may obtain salvation. The sacraments present the concrete, tangible, and real means by which Christ desires to accomplish our salvation and therefore must be an indispensable part of our efforts of evangelization. Pope Paul VI focused on this point in his papal exhortation:

> The search for God himself through prayer which is principally that of adoration and thanksgiving, but also through communion with the visible sign of the encounter with God which is the Church of Jesus Christ; and this communion in its turn is expressed by the application of those other signs of Christ living and acting in the Church which are the sacraments. To live the sacraments in this way, bringing their celebration to a true fullness, is not, as some would claim, to impede or to accept a distortion of evangelization: it is rather to complete it. For in its totality, evangelization—over and above the preaching of a message—consists in the implantation of the Church, which does not exist without the driving force which is the sacramental life culminating in the Eucharist.[24]

The saints stand first and foremost as our models of embodying the sacraments themselves, while at the same time pointing and leading others to the depths of these mysteries.

Three years before the French Revolution, a holy witness was born that would become an inspiration to parish priests from that time. Many perceived **St. Jean Vianney** (1786–1859) to be below average in about every worldly way one could imagine; however, he excelled extraordinarily when it came to holiness and evangelization. When Jean became the pastor of Ars, a typical French village of the nineteenth century, worldly devotion and lackluster religious passion consumed it. It became the new pastor's opinion that the parish would not be considered "converted" until every single parishioner was living according to the commandments, precepts of the Church, and a sacramental life. This desire consumed his thoughts: "My God, grant me the conversion of my parish; I am willing to suffer all my life whatsoever it may please thee to lay upon me; yes, even for a hundred years am I prepared to endure the sharpest pains, only let my people be converted." How could such a noble mission be fulfilled?

While every sacrament cooperates in the work of evangelization, Jean Vianney lived and breathed two sacraments in particular—the Blessed Sacrament and confession. Numerous stories have been told about the countless hours that Jean toiled in the confessional and how pilgrims from all around France stood in line to receive the sacrament from the saint. However, it was the Blessed Sacrament that Jean would draw his strength from. He celebrated Mass with a passion that gave parishioners a glimpse of the heavenly realities the liturgy signifies. Eucharistic Adoration centered Jean's life and evangelization efforts. He established Forty Hours Devotion at the parish. Once when an older man was sitting for so long in front of the Eucharistic Lord in the tabernacle, Jean inquired what he did for so many hours. "I look at him, and he looks at me," the devout man responded. If we have hopes of bringing the Gospel to loved ones or to strangers, we must be a Eucharistic people. Our ability to see and love the Savior of the World under the appearance of bread and wine develops and nourishes our ability to see and love the lost and be effective instruments of the Gospel.

St. John Baptist de Rossi (1698–1764), a holy Italian priest, became renowned not for his charismatic personality or preaching but because of the work he did to heal the broken, both physically and spiritually. John Baptist spent forty years working in hospitals tending to the sick. For the first several years of his priesthood, John refused to hear confessions, perhaps because of his extreme shyness. Fortunately for the good of the people, a friend convinced St. John to exercise this faculty of reconciliation; and indeed, this was where his priesthood blossomed. With only simple directions from the saint in the confessional, people's lives were transformed. These experiences of conversions in the sacrament of reconciliation led John to remark, "I used often to wonder what was the shortest road to heaven. It lies in guiding others there through the confessional…. What a power for good that can be!" This calling exists for the laity too! We must strive to bring others to the doors of mercy, the doors of a confessional. We cannot mandate or impose but simply invite and propose.

A young man dying of syphilis would have nothing to do with the Catholic priest who wanted to speak with him about the prospects of eternity. Until one day, moved by John Baptist empting his bedpan, he broke down and conversed honestly with the saint. John heard the young man's confession before he passed away of his illness. What a beautiful image of the work of bringing others to Mercy. That bedpan could be a symbol of our willingness to get into the messiness of other people's lives. The work of evangelization often involves rolling up our sleeves and getting into the muck and muddiness that often are a part of life. It is not always a clean job, but it is our job. We must be willing to draw near to one's brokenness in order to usher them to the Divine Physician. The underpinnings of evangelization mirror very much the work of an usher; to walk with someone in order to put them into a position to see whom they really need to see. Once we have brought them to the Font of Mercy, we can trust that the One who loves them most will bring them home to his merciful arms.

The most decorated chaplain in United States history was servant of God *Fr. Emil Kapaun* (1916–1951). Born surrounded by wheat fields in Pilsen, Kansas, he is now on the road to being a canonized saint. Fr. Emil left the work of a diocesan parish priest to become a chaplain for the U.S. Army, which led him to the center of the Korean War. Eventually captured, he suffered with other soldiers who were held in a concentration camp for almost two years. During this time he cared for each of "his boys'" physical and spiritual needs. The soldiers, when possible, procured some crumbs of bread and a little wine to allow their chaplain to celebrate the Eucharist. When Chaplain Kapaun entered your presence, no matter how filthy the hut, it became a cathedral, with the nearness of God being undeniable. The harsh conditions of the camp and the abuse he received from his captors eventually wore down Fr. Kapaun's body. His captors carried him to the death house as he spoke, "Forgive them, Father." Fr. Emil Kapaun gave his life in order to bring the sacraments to the soldiers. One of the most famous pictures of the chaplain is him celebrating Mass on the hood of a Jeep for one lone soldier in a field.

Before being shipped off to the Korean War, Fr. Kapaun was stationed at Fort Bliss, Texas, in 1948. There he received a new bunk mate, Orzo Barclay. Orzo, an Episcopalian, was dating a young Catholic woman. He had thought about talking to a chaplain about the difference in religion, but he never anticipated he would be living with one. Orzo's suspicions of Catholics were confirmed when he opened the door to his new quarters to be greeted by a huge picture of the Blessed Virgin Mary. Over time Fr. Kapaun and Orzo became close friends. The chaplain's kindness and gentleness opened Orzo to conversations about the sacrament of marriage and the Catholic faith. Fr. Kapaun used the prospect of the approaching sacrament of marriage to bring Orzo into the Catholic Church.

Every sacrament has a role in our salvation, but every sacrament is also a moment of evangelization. Whether it is a marriage, a couple bringing their baby to be baptized, a couple bringing their child for First Communion, or a young person seeking to be confirmed, these are opportunities, sacred moments, to bring them to a deeper encounter with Jesus Christ. Perhaps an opportunity presents itself to invite a neighbor or coworker to a baptism or First Communion—what a monumental opening to display the beauty of the Church. We individually and collectively in a parish must be prepared for these precious sacred moments so that we do not let them pass by without fruit of the New Evangelization.

One of the great examples of good things coming in small packages is the five-foot superhero *St. Teresa of Calcutta* (1910–1997). Most of us blessed to live in her lifetime have our favorite memories of this incredible woman. The pictures of St. Teresa with Pope St. John Paul II express the unbelievable joy that each one possessed. The other memory I will never forget: St. Teresa's speech at the 1994 National Prayer Breakfast, when she implored, "Anybody who doesn't want their child, please give it to me. I want the child." This boldness led to extraordinary accomplishments. She started out with twelve sisters; by the time of her death, there were more than 4,000 Missionaries of Charity sisters operating 610 foundations in 123 countries.

In the midst of those accomplishments, Teresa pointed to the simple basic principles of how they were accomplished. For instance, when she won the Noble Peace Prize, Mother Teresa was asked how we can gain world peace. Her simple response was, "Go home and love your family." The real secret to all her success lay in the sacraments. At a point when the sisters of the Missionaries of Charity were experiencing major growing pains, Mother Teresa added something to their life that insured the order's continued fruitfulness. The sisters were overwhelmed with balancing their work and spiritual commitments. At the time, they would do a Holy Hour in front of the Blessed Sacrament once a week. Mother Teresa instituted daily Holy Hours for each of the sisters. From that time on, she testified, they had more vocations, more time for work, and even more money to distribute to the poor. When she was asked what would save America and the world, Mother Teresa responded from her learned experience: "Holy Hours."

Like St. Teresa, we at times feel exhaustion and perhaps despair settle into our evangelization efforts. We begin to feel that all of our hard work has produced little fruit. It is precisely in these moments that we must recommit to drawing closer to the sacraments. These sacraments, especially the Eucharist, are the source and the goal of evangelization. Our desire must be to lead others to experience the Eucharistic Lord, but this will only be accomplished if we are a Eucharistic people. The sacraments constantly remind us that the work of evangelization is not *our* work but *his* work. Jesus wants to feed the hungry and give drink to the thirsty. We must bring the hungry and thirsty to his eternal banquet table.

ST. MARTIN OF TOURS

ST. EPHREM

ST. ANGELA MERICI

ST. BERNARD OF CLAIRVAUX

Pillar 6

FORMATIONAL

The Lord's missionary mandate includes a call to growth in faith: "Teach them to observe all that I have commanded you" (Mt 28:20). Hence it is clear that the first proclamation also calls for ongoing formation and maturation. Evangelization aims at a process of growth which entails taking seriously each person and God's plan for his or her life. All of us need to grow in Christ. Evangelization should stimulate a desire for this growth, so that each of us can say wholeheartedly: "It is no longer I who live, but Christ who lives in me" (Gal 2:20).

— Pope Francis [25]

In thirteen years of teaching in Catholic schools, I have noticed a trend within the students who graduate. The overwhelming majority of them will cease studying anything about their faith. Somewhere along the line they acquired the notion that once their formal education was complete, so was their faith formation. Such a notion is simply not true. It is not true for our children, nor is it true for adults. There will never come a time when we know everything there is to be known about the faith. So parishes, dioceses, and other institutions must provide solid catechesis. In recent decades many great resources have been made available for such formal catechetical instruction.

As important as formal education is, formation cannot be understood solely as what takes place at a desk, with an educator, or in a formal setting. Pope Francis shares with us:

> It would not be right to see this call to growth exclusively or primarily in terms of doctrinal formation. It has to do with "observing" all that the Lord has shown us as the way of responding to his love. Along with the virtues, this means above all the new commandment, the first and the greatest of the commandments, and the one that best identifies us as Christ's disciples: "This is my commandment, that you love one another as I have loved you" (Jn 15:12).[26]

Yes, the knowledge of doctrine, commandments, precepts, beatitudes, and everything considered catechesis remains essential to formation. But more important is the application of how this knowledge is lived out daily. How is the eighth commandment applied to the workplace? What does it look like to love our enemies? What does it mean to be open to life? This form of education is not learned in a classroom, but instead by Christians living and journeying together, modeling the Christian life to one another. Christ exemplifies this formation with his apostles, and the saints have striven for two thousand years to continue the method of formation.

In the first three centuries of the Church, becoming a saint was almost as easy as getting baptized, because when people chose to receive baptism, they also chose to put their names on a short list for martyrdom. One of the first recognized saints without the crown of martyrdom is **St. Martin of Tours** (316–397). As a Roman soldier, Martin never once used his sword. As a monk seeking solicitude, Martin became a bishop against his own desires. As a bishop preaching against the heresy of the times, he sought mercy for the heretics. Many sought capital punishment for such heretics; and yet Martin, even though his enemies had exiled him, still believed clemency should be shown. Martin lived during a time when nowhere near the majority of the population was Christian, so he knew that evangelization could not take place in his cathedral with his preaching alone. Martin instead undertook a program of evangelization that proved to be more personal and more time-consuming. He journeyed from house to house to engage people with the Gospel. Once he had a number of converts, he arranged them in communities, with a priest responsible for their formation. Martin would then visit them as a shepherd caring for his sheep.

Seventeen hundred years later this method of evangelization still remains essential. As our culture becomes more nonreligious, we must admit that the people we long to reach are not necessarily going to come into our churches on Sunday. However, they live across the street and greet us as neighbors. Our everyday encounters at work, at the ballpark, or in our neighborhood challenge us to an opportunity for formation and evangelization. Pope Francis emphasizes these opportunities:

> Today, as the Church seeks to experience a profound missionary renewal, there is a kind of preaching which falls to each of us as a daily responsibility. It has to do with bringing the Gospel to the people we meet, whether they be our neighbors or complete strangers. This is the informal preaching which takes place in the middle of a conversation, something along the lines of what a missionary does when visiting a home. Being a disciple means being constantly ready to bring the love of Jesus to others, and this can happen unexpectedly and in any place: on the street, in a city square, during work, on a journey.[27]

"Family to family evangelization" provides one of the most effective natural methods of evangelization and formation. It is one thing to be built up and nourished in Mass or on the campuses of our churches, but we can walk this Christian walk with one another in the very neighborhoods in which we live.

Another witness to the effectiveness of formation in people's homes is **St. Angela Merici** (1474–1540). She knew what it was to have the deck stacked against her. Her parents died at an early age, and her guardian uncle died when she was only twenty. Without a formal education, Angela managed to learn on her own. She then began to achieve success teaching the young girls of the wealthy class. At that time, education existed only for the rich and religious. The impetus to educate women or the poor, sadly, is a modern notion. Angela knew the problems facing the poor and young girls as well as the obstacles to overcoming them. Women could not be teachers, and an unmarried woman by herself in the public square was unacceptable. Some of the women educated at the time were religious sisters; however, they could not leave the convent.

To answer the need for formation for these unfortunate young girls, Angela gathered around her twelve young women. She formed them to form others. Angela commissioned them to wherever the young girls were able to teach and form. She called this group the Company of St. Ursula, patroness of medieval universities. The group grew to twenty-eight women; by the time of Angela's death they had multiplied to twenty-four communities. Shortly after her death, the association she formed officially became the Ursuline Sisters, the first and still one of the largest women religious teaching orders. What a great example of getting outside the box when it comes to formation! Our goal becomes living Christian lives not merely while at church but wherever we live. Why not have our book or Bible studies in our homes? Or better yet, why not have them at our workplaces? Instead of using our lunch hours for break time, is there someone we can share lunch with in order to build one another up in this Christian walk? We must begin to see formation as something more than what happens on Sunday, Wednesday, or at church. Formation will happen "where two or three are gathered in my name, there am I in the midst of them" (Mt 18:20).

Known as "The Harp of the Holy Spirit," **St. Ephrem** (ca. 306–373) is the only Syrian officially recognized as one of the thirty-six Doctors of the Church. Surrounded by political upheaval and heresies raging against the Church, Ephrem stood as a light in the darkness. He became a prolific writer of hymns and prose. Four hundred hymns still exist today composed by his creative mind. He stands as one of the most influential persons in awakening the Church to the use of music and poetry to spread the faith. His compositions were a response to the heresies of the time. He was concerned, as was St. Paul during his own time, that people were "tossed to and fro and carried about with every wind of doctrine, by the cunning of men, by their craftiness in deceitful wiles" (Eph 4:14). The heretics placed their false doctrines in song with beautiful music so that people would be captivated and remember the teachings. Imagining the influence that music and the modern media of one's culture has in leading people away from the Truth of salvation is not difficult.

In response, Ephrem took the melodies of the popular songs of the time and composed new lyrics that taught the orthodox beliefs of the Church. He used images from the Judeo-Christian background but also incorporated Greek philosophy and cultural references that would be familiar for those listening. In other words, he used the tools of the culture to teach Eternal Truth. Ephrem had no difficulty meeting people where they were in their formation. Do we do the same with our methods of formation and pedagogy? Imagine what Ephrem would do with today's modern means of communication. It is not enough that we use radio, music, television, the Internet, and social networks, but we must learn to use them well and often. People consume information today in this manner, so this precisely where our formation in Christ must also exist.

It is not often that one person stands out among all the rest as the most important and influential of a century; however, the first half of the twelfth century had such a person in **St. Bernard of Clairvaux** (1090–1153). In his lifetime Bernard founded more than sixty new Cistercian monasteries, with hundreds to follow after his death. Bernard's astounding influence on bishops, abbots, secular rulers, and even popes resonated beyond the time in which he lived. Still influencing the Church today, he stands as a Doctor of the Church, known as the *Doctor Mellifluus* or Honey-sweet Doctor. Even when he was young, it became evident that Bernard desired holiness, and people were willing to follow him in that pursuit. After Bernard lived at the monastery in Citeaux, France, for only three short years, the abbot sent him along with twelve other men to establish a new monastery. This new monastery became the world-famous Clairvaux. However, its beginning was a difficult one.

The land was difficult, so all the monks had to eat was barley bread and roots to substitute for vegetables. It did not help that the young abbot, Bernard, was severe in expecting his brother monks to follow the rule as he did. Eventually the saint noticed that the monks had become discouraged. The saint in his humility recognized his fault and lightened the discipline for the monks. They grew in holiness, and in a short time their numbers grew to more than one hundred thirty. What an important lesson to learn in our efforts of formation! We cannot overwhelm new converts with doctrinal and moral formation in the first moments of their conversion. St. Paul recognized this within his work at Corinth, "I fed you with milk, not solid food; for you were not ready for it; and even yet you are not ready" (1 Cor 3:2). No, we must not water down the faith, but simply discern where someone is in their faith journey and give them what they need to fruitfully continue the walk.

The need for genuine formation, both in the traditional catechetical settings and in the classroom of life, are vital to the work of the New Evangelization. We must be willing to meet people where they are whether that is in our home, their home, work, or a sports arena. The formation must occur there because it is precisely where Christians must live as Christians. To reach this generation, we must also be able to use modern means of communication well. The Gospel is meant to be a light in the darkness, even if that is on the Internet. By discerning what level of formation people are ready for, we will be able to send them out to forming others. They will be ready to carry this mission.

Pillar 7

MISSIONFUL

Every Christian is a missionary to the extent that he or she has encountered the love of God in Christ Jesus: we no longer say that we are "disciples" and "missionaries," but rather that we are always "missionary disciples." If we are not convinced, let us look at those first disciples, who, immediately after encountering the gaze of Jesus, went forth to proclaim him joyfully: "We have found the Messiah!" (Jn 1:41). The Samaritan woman became a missionary immediately after speaking with Jesus and many Samaritans come to believe in him "because of the woman's testimony" (Jn 4:39). So too, Saint Paul, after his encounter with Jesus Christ, "immediately proclaimed Jesus" (Acts 9:20; cf. 22:6–21). So what are we waiting for?

— Pope Francis [28]

The most powerful sending forth in human history occurs in the Gospel of Matthew: the Great Commission (Mt 28:18–20). Jesus does not send the disciples out with the good news to make believers, but instead commands his disciples to "make disciples." An important circular logic is present in this command. Jesus emphatically commands the disciples to make disciples. Therefore, "someone who makes disciples"

69

becomes a necessary component to the definition of a disciple. This process has continued ever since the Great Commission, and we know this because you and I have caught the faith from someone. Pope Francis reflects about how this exact work played out in the ministry of St. Paul:

> Genuine spiritual accompaniment always begins and flourishes in the context of service to the mission of evangelization. Paul's relationship with Timothy and Titus provides an example of this accompaniment and formation which takes place in the midst of apostolic activity. Entrusting them with the mission of remaining in each city to "put in order what remains to be done" (Tit 1:5; cf.1 Tim 1:3–5), Paul also gives them rules for their personal lives and their pastoral activity. This is clearly distinct from every kind of intrusive accompaniment or isolated self-realization. Missionary disciples accompany missionary disciples.[29]

Therefore, if we have prayed for, invited, and welcomed the lost; inspired them with the authentic message of Christ and brought them to the sacraments; and walked with them to form them in the Christian life; our efforts will not be complete until we have sent them out as missionary disciples equipped to share this new life they have discovered. The saints of the Church are disciple-making machines.

The second canonized saint who was born in America, **St. Katharine Drexel** (1858–1955), has an amazing story of riches to rags to an eternal reward. Katharine's father, Francis Drexel, was a successful banker who became one of the richest men in America. Her biological mother died shortly after giving birth to Katharine, so she was raised by Emma Bouvier, Francis's second wife. Along with their immense wealth, the Drexels had immense faith. Katharine's father would pray a half hour every evening, and the family would open up their house to the poor three times a week for food and clothing. Emma would take Katharine and her sisters out to find those who needed help but would not or could not come to the family home. When Katharine's father passed away, she and her two sisters split an inheritance that was worth, in today's dollars, over $400,000,000. Katharine immediately began to send money to ministries working with Native Americans, for whom she developed an empathy during her family travels.

Something powerful was stirring in Katharine. On a trip to Europe she had the chance to meet Pope Leo XIII. Katharine pleaded with the pope to send more missionaries to work with the Native American and black communities in America. Pope Leo responded, "Why don't you become a missionary?" Two years after that visit, Katharine entered the convent. Two years later she established a new religious order called the Sisters of the Blessed Sacrament, commissioned to work with the Native American and black populations. Katharine had a major heart attack at the age of seventy-seven, which necessitated giving up leadership of the order, but by that time she had established 145 missions, 12 schools for Native American students, 50 schools for black students, and the first black Catholic college—Xavier University in New Orleans, Louisiana. Katharine answered the personal call to make disciples. She realized it was not enough to simply give money to support missionaries, even though that is a necessary and great act of charity; but also that she must personally bring the Gospel to all within her power. We must follow this call too. Whether we have millions of dollars or are penniless, we can bring the Gospel to the lost, right now where we are.

The central component to effective evangelization begins with the pursuit of holiness. In the last one hundred years, perhaps no one has done more to promote the call to personal holiness than **St. Josemaria Escriva** (1902–1975). On October 2, 1928, when Josemaria lived as a young priest in Madrid, Spain, he received a divine mission to begin Opus Dei. Opus Dei exists as an organization made up of laity and priests dedicated to seeking holiness in everyday, ordinary life, exactly where they are in their workplaces and neighborhoods. For those of us raised after Vatican II, this may not be such a startling message, but in the first half of the twentieth century it was not commonplace. In fact, Josemaria and his work may have had a great deal to do with the Second Vatican Council making this kind of statement:

> All the faithful of Christ of whatever rank or status, are called to the fullness of the Christian life and to the perfection of charity; by this holiness as such a more human manner of living is promoted in this earthly society. In order that the faithful may reach this perfection, they must use their strength accordingly as they have received it, as a gift from Christ. They must follow in His footsteps and conform themselves to His image seeking the will of the Father in all things. They must devote themselves with all their being to the glory of God and the service of their neighbor. In this way, the holiness of the People of God will grow into an abundant harvest of good, as is admirably shown by the life of so many saints in Church history.[30]

Today, Opus Dei boasts nearly one hundred thousand members in more than ninety countries seeking a radical call to holiness in their everyday work and lives.

After receiving the mission from the Lord, Josemaria set about gathering young people around him from the university. He would walk with them, have coffee, or take them on trips to help the poor. When it was time for a more formal catechetical formation, he invited many to the first class. Only three showed up, but the saint was undeterred. While Josemaria blessed the three students with Eucharistic Benediction, he had a vision of a crowd of three hundred, then three hundred thousand, on up to three billion all over the world. Josemaria sent those three disciples out to seek holiness and to create disciples by loving their neighbors. That became the force for holiness that is Opus Dei today.

So often churches today get caught up in numbers. Programs and events are based on the amount of money they cost and the number of people they brought in. When I speak around the country, parishioners often tell me, "Oh, I wish everyone in the parish could have heard this message," or "There should have been more people at the mission." But are numbers the best gauge of valuation? After three years of ministry, Jesus ended up on a cross with only his mother, one disciple, and two women standing by him. Most parish committees would have judged that program to be a failure. If we have three disciples, then send them out. If they are true disciples, then they will create more disciples, and soon will see multiplications beyond our dreams. The multiplications will not be just attendees to events, but they also will be authentic disciples ready for the mission of the Gospel.

Being the wealthy nephew of a pope would have its advantages in the sixteenth century—unless holiness and reformation are on your mind, of course. **St. Charles Borromeo** (1538–1584) was appointed a cardinal by his uncle Pope Pius IV while Charles was still in his teen years and a layman. Eventually, Charles would become Archbishop of Milan and transform the diocese into a shining star for others to model during the time of the turbulent Protestant Reformation. He spearheaded the reopening of the Council of Trent and its concluding proceedings. When famine and sickness struck Milan and the wealthy fled, Charles stayed. He fed and cared for the sick personally and out of his own financial resources. His work ethic and perhaps the plague would catch up to Charles, taking this model bishop away from the Church while he was still in his forties.

Charles believed two of the major problems that brought on the Protestant Reformation were priests who were ignorant of Church teachings and laity who were not catechized. To correct the first problem, Charles established what would become the modern-day seminary system. To correct the second problem, he created the Confraternity of Christian Doctrine—or, as it is still known in many parishes, CCD. But for Charles, CCD was a very specific evangelization game plan. First he gathered laymen for the purposes of teaching catechism to children. Charles was confident that if these loyal laymen taught the faith as if they were missionaries, their own personal faith would catch on fire. Charles called them "Fishers," and they wore the badge of a fisherman. However, this plan was more involved. Once the children were educated, what would they do with their newfound faith? The children brought it home to Mom and Dad. By this simple, missionful concept of evangelization, St. Charles turned his diocese completely around. To see our own parishes, workplaces, and communities as mission fields forces us to find new avenues and perhaps new disciples to bring the Gospel to the lost.

A book on the topic of saints and the New Evangelization would be pretty incomplete without a story about *Pope St. John Paul the Great* (1920–2005). He in fact is the person who gave us the term "New Evangelization" and promised that it would bring about a new springtime of the faith. Almost everything that John Paul brought to his work as an effective evangelizing pope he learned during his time as a priest and bishop in Poland. While under totalitarian regimes, John Paul could not speak to the masses through radio, print, or even the public square. So he used personal relationships. John Paul would go on camping trips in the mountains with young people, not to preach to them but to listen and dialogue. Through these methods, John Paul was laying a foundation that would soon change the face of Poland.

I have attempted to stay away from personal stories and instead share saints' stories to teach the Pillars and Characteristics. However, this story involves both. The only time I saw Pope John Paul II was at World Youth Day in 1993. It was the summer before my senior year of high school. At that point in my life I was not in a good place when it came to my faith. Being self-absorbed, I was more interested in meeting girls from Spain than in meeting the pope. Yet, I can still remember John Paul entering Mile High Stadium. The love of Christ through John Paul filled the stadium. Even though my life was steeped in sin at the time, it brought tears to my eyes. A couple of years would pass before my conversion from sin to living the Catholic faith would be complete, but I have no doubts that being in St. John Paul II's presence had an impact. I am amazed at how many people from my generation who are now active in their faith were there as well. My wife was in Denver, even though we did not meet then. My good friends Jason Evert and Chris Stefanick were there in 1993, but we did not meet. (I guess because they were not girls from Spain.) I know many priests who were also at that event as teens and young adults. The full impact will probably never be known this side of heaven.

If we want to do something radical to grow our faith, then we must share the faith. If you want someone's faith to come to life, encourage them to share the faith. Send them out. Embolden them to be missionaries. Pope St. John Paul the Great challenged the young people at World Youth Day in 1993 to be just that—to be missionaries:

At this stage of history, the liberating message of the Gospel of life has been put into your hands. And the mission of proclaiming it to the ends of the earth is now passing to your generation. Like the great Apostle Paul, you too must feel the full urgency of the task: "Woe to me if I do not evangelize" (1 Cor 9:16).

Preaching the Gospel changed the world two thousand years ago and every day since. If we are convicted of that Truth, then there is hope for our family, friends, country, and world that is beyond all measure.

Part Two

The Saints and the
Seven Characteristics
of an Effective
Evangelist

BL. PIER GIORGIO FRASSATI

BL. CHIARA BADANO

ST. JOSEPHINE BAKHITA

ST. PHILIP NERI

Characteristic 1

JOYFUL

The Gospel joy which enlivens the community of disciples is a missionary joy. The seventy-two disciples felt it as they returned from their mission (cf. Lk 10:17). Jesus felt it when he rejoiced in the Holy Spirit and praised the Father for revealing himself to the poor and the little ones (cf. Lk 10:21). It was felt by the first converts who marveled to hear the apostles preaching "in the native language of each" (Acts 2:6) on the day of Pentecost. This joy is a sign that the Gospel has been proclaimed and is bearing fruit.

— Pope Francis [31]

The Bible mentions the words "joy" or "rejoicing" more than five hundred times, excluding other words that could be associated with joy such as gladness or happiness. Obviously, joy ought to play a crucial role in the life of every Christian. Stop and imagine what emotions the disciples experienced when they saw the Risen Lord. As Scripture describes it, "they worshiped him, and returned to Jerusalem with *great joy*" (Lk 24:52, emphasis added). Great joy? Can two words even begin to capture the emotion they experienced on that day? That great joy has been passed down to us two thousand years later. But our joy is not just a residue left over from some historical event. If we stand as authentic Christians, then we have encountered Jesus, which ought to produce an authentic joy. When strangers enter our churches or our homes, do they see and experience that same joy? Pope Francis fears this joy is lacking: "There are Christians whose lives seem like Lent without Easter. I realize of course that joy is not expressed the same way at all times in life, especially at moments of great difficulty. Joy adapts and changes, but it always endures, even as a flicker of light born of our personal certainty that, when everything is said and done, we are infinitely loved."[32] Clearly, true joy is not authenticated by some pie-in-the-sky, everything-is-roses-and-rainbows outlook. As Christians, our life is characterized by the crosses and sufferings we bear. The saints were able to maintain joy in both the crown of triumph and the cross, and that joy became contagious for those who encountered them.

While we should admire all the saints for their virtue and strong faith, some, like **Blessed Pier Giorgio Frassati** (1901–1925), seemed to have it all. Pier Giorgio was born in Turin, Italy, into a life of luxury. His parents were extraordinarily wealthy. In fact, of all the homes they owned, the smallest boasted thirty-six rooms. His father, Alfredo, founded the newspaper *La Stampa,* which remains in publication to this day. At one point, he also was an ambassador to Germany. But as an atheist, Alfredo did not consider faith a part of his luxurious lifestyle; and while Pier's mother attended church, she was never seen taking Communion, nor were prayers ever said in the house. Yet the grace of God reached Pier Giorgio to turn him into a light in the darkness. He became a champion skier, mountain climber, political activist, and student. People wanted to be around Pier Giorgio, not just because he was an athletic, good-looking, rich young man, but because he had a smile that could light up a room thanks to authentic joy.

Like most young people, Pier Giorgio treasured his friends and the time he spent with them. Yet whether it was a ski trip or a mountain climbing expedition, he would only go if a Catholic Church stood nearby or if a priest could go with them. He desired to go to Mass, and he would bring his friends along. They would say that while their parents or priests could not get them to go to Mass, Pier Giorgio could. The close group of friends ironically called themselves "The Sinister Ones." They could be heard laughing and playing practical jokes on one another. Pier Giorgio would challenge them to a game of pool. The wager would be money or going to Eucharistic Adoration for an hour with him. Good thing he was a talented pool player. As the loud group of friends would enter the chapel, they quietly went into the pews. Pier Giorgio would distribute prayers; after spending his hour kneeling in front of the Eucharist, he would gather his friends (waking some of them up), and they would be back on their way to a fun-filled evening.

Joy is contagious. People want to be around joyful people. Often there's a subconscious question: "Why are they so joyful?" So many of Pier Giorgio's friends asked that question. Even Pope St. John Paul II was influenced by his joy. In 1989, Pope John Paul visited the original tomb of Pier Giorgio in Pollone, Italy. He said, "I, too, in my youth, felt the beneficial influence of his example and, as a student, I was impressed by the force of his testimony."[33] If our joy is authentic, it will become contagious, and perhaps it will make an impression on a future pope someday.

God calls followers from every economic situation. *St. Josephine Bakhita* (1869–1947) certainly was not raised in the lap of luxury. Josephine was born in Sudan but kidnapped by Arab slave traders around the age of nine. She was bought and sold multiple times and forced to convert to Islam. Harsh owners beat her regularly, leaving her with 144 scars. Eventually she was purchased by a merchant, Callisto Legnani, who took Josephine to Italy. For the first time, Josephine came to know a master who did not use a whip but instead was gentle and kind and treated her with respect. Through a series of circumstances, Legnani gave custody of Josephine to some friends, the Michieli family. It was with them that Josephine met the Canossian Sisters, who introduced her to the Master above all masters.

Josephine, through the grace of God, joined the Canossian Sisters. In her time as a religious, her gentle smile never left her. Perhaps it is for this reason that she was given the responsibility of doorkeeper, because every person was greeted with her smile. Her fellow sisters called Josephine their "Black Mother," and she took on the duties of cook and sacristan. Josephine now found joy in her service in a completely new way. "A committed missionary knows the joy of being a spring which spills over and refreshes others," Pope Francis says. "Only the person who feels happiness in seeking the good of others, in desiring their happiness, can be a missionary. This openness of the heart is a source of joy."[34]

One of the most inspiring stories of the second half of the twentieth century is that of *Blessed Chiara "Luce" Badano* (1971–1990). This teenager exemplified normal in every sense of the word except when it came to her extraordinary faith. Chiara was reared in a devout Catholic family in Italy. As a little girl she was faithful, and in her teenage years Chiara gave her life entirely to Jesus Christ. Yet, she still loved her friends and sports. She excelled at mountain climbing, swimming, and tennis. Chiara also had a heart for sharing the Gospel. She described evangelizing her friends "by the way I listen to them, by the way I dress, and above all, by the way I love them." Chiara was popular and dreamt of being a flight attendant — and her smile would have made the longest flights enjoyable. At the age of seventeen, however, Chiara was diagnosed with osteogenic sarcoma, an incurable bone cancer.

From the beginning, Chiara's prognosis was not good, and yet she suffered with a smile. She refused morphine in order to have more to offer up to Jesus and be mentally available to visitors. It was during these trials that she was given the nickname "Luce," which means "light," because her joy shined through her failing body. A cardinal who heard of this exceptional teenager visited Chiara and asked her where the light in her eyes came from. She responded, "I try to love Jesus as much as I can." Chiara's last words were "Goodbye, be happy. I'm happy." If anyone had an excuse not to be joyful it could certainly have been Chiara, but that is not how saints operate. Pope Francis reflected on this:

> Sometimes we are tempted to find excuses and complain, acting as if we could only be happy if a thousand conditions were met. To some extent this is because our "technological society has succeeded in multiplying occasions of pleasure, yet has found it very difficult to engender joy." I can say that the most beautiful and natural expressions of joy which I have seen in my life were in poor people who had little to hold on to.[35]

Joy in the midst of trials and suffering is so indescribably attractive to those who witness it. It could be that in the moments of pain or crisis our ability to reach the lost is greater. That pervades the reality with the saints and with Jesus's own suffering and death.

At a time when the city of Rome was once again in need of spiritual reformation, God brought into their midst **St. Philip Neri** (1515–1595), "The Second Apostle of Rome." After a conversion to a deeper faith in his late teens, Philip left the businessman path to go to Rome. There he spent time praying and working with the poor and sick, as well as with pilgrims in the streets of the Eternal City. Philip's spiritual director, after seeing the success of his efforts, convinced him to become a priest. Eventually he formed the Roman Congregation of the Oratory. While it is not a religious order, it gathered men in a common way of life marked with a distinct spirituality and way of spreading the Gospel. What so easily attracted people to Philip was his wit, humor, and joy. Pope Francis said, "An evangelizer must never look like someone who has just come back from a funeral!"[36] Philip is a great example of this teaching, as he would say, "A joyful heart is more easily made perfect than a downcast one." His joy was present even in correcting people's faults. When a repentant man asked Philip if wearing a hair shirt would be a good form of penance, the saint responded that it would only if he wore it on the outside of his clothes. Philip's wit covered difficult subjects, even that of humility.

Over time Philip gained a great reputation, obviously amongst the poor but even with cardinals, bishops, and the wealthy. A man invited Philip to a party that in today's terms would be considered an A-list event. It was to be for Rome's "who's who." It was incredibly awkward for the guests when Philip arrived with half of his beard neatly trimmed and the other half shaved off. Every time I think of this story, I can imagine the horror my wife would go through if I left the house like this. Philip did not have a wife, but he did spend the entire evening conversing with the host of the party, so that Rome's celebrities could see him with the half-beard man. While I am confident there was a personal message of humility from Philip to all at the party, I believe there is something deeper.

How foolish must Philip have looked with half of a beard! For those who saw it, there could only be two conclusions. Either this Philip really is a living saint, or he is a man gone mad. I have a feeling that the majority of Christians fear being called a saint or a lunatic. Either we are afraid of people thinking we are "holier than thou," or thinking that we are "nuts." Like St. Paul, Philip embraced the absurdity of Christianity. "We preach Christ crucified, a stumbling block to Jews and folly to Gentiles.... For the foolishness of God is wiser than men" (1 Cor 1:23, 25). Christianity is different, Christians are to be different; but this different life lived with authentic joy becomes what is so attractive to those in the world.

As missionary disciples, we are called to be "fishers of men." There is no better lure than joy when it comes to catching souls. But our joy must be authentic, not a shallow happiness. Our joy must be ever-present, even in the midst of suffering. The saints have taught us that the world can take our money, our things, and even our pleasures away, but the world cannot take our joy. Our joy is in Christ and serves as the testimony to his abiding presence.

ST. FRANCES
XAVIER CABRINI

ST. LAWRENCE
GIVSTINIANI

ST. HOSPITIVS

ST. PIVS V

Characteristic 2

HUMBLE

The world which, paradoxically, despite innumerable signs of the denial of God, is nevertheless searching for Him in unexpected ways and painfully experiencing the need of Him—the world is calling for evangelizers to speak to it of a God whom the evangelists themselves should know and be familiar with as if they could see the invisible. The world calls for and expects from us simplicity of life, the spirit of prayer, charity towards all, especially towards the lowly and the poor, obedience and humility, detachment and self-sacrifice. Without this mark of holiness, our word will have difficulty in touching the heart of modern man. It risks being vain and sterile.

— Pope Paul VI [37]

The virtue of humility is difficult to master, and the moment that you think, "I really got this humility thing down," you fall back into pride. Humility is one of those virtues that we love to see in others; we are annoyed when it is not present. Yet, we rarely are as concerned if it is or is not present in us. In our success-driven, "you can do anything you set your mind to" culture today it becomes challenging, to say the least, for parents to teach humility to their children. Perhaps today, many would not see humility as a virtue at all but a weakness. They harbor a false understanding of humility as thinking less of oneself. However, humility is knowing who you are in the sight of God, a sinner who is loved and redeemed. The saints were indeed people who knew who they were in God and with God. The humble saints carried the Truth of the Gospel with a gentle strength that could not be ignored.

A woman exemplifying humility as strength and not a weakness is *St. Frances Xavier Cabrini* (1850–1917). Mother Cabrini, as she is affectionately known in America, entered the world very humbly and small—literally, she was born two months premature. In her youth, she fought constant health problems, yet Frances believed she was a daughter of God called to extraordinary things. One of her favorite pastimes was to build toy boats and pretend to sail them to China, where she could be a missionary. By her late teens Frances desired to be a religious, but because of health concerns she was unable. Instead she worked at an orphanage. When the orphanage closed, Frances gathered six like-minded women and founded the Missionary Sisters of the Sacred Heart. Realization of her childhood dream had finally taken root. However, in her humility Frances submitted her order to the good of the Church. While meeting with Pope Leo XIII, she asked if he desired for the order to go to China. Leo answered, "Not to the east, but to the west." Frances did as she was directed.

When Mother Cabrini arrived in New York City, neither the orphanage building nor the bishop were available. In fact, Frances was told to go back to Italy. Filled with equal parts tenacity and faith, she knew who she was and stayed the course true to her calling. Her strength existed in her humble submission to the will of God. When others asked her to take over a failing hospital, Frances refused, believing it was beyond her skills. That night, however, she had a dream of the

Blessed Mother assuring her that this indeed was God's will. Humbly, she accepted. In thirty-five years her order established sixty-seven school, hospitals, and orphanages across the United States, Europe, and South America, despite the fact that Frances never really mastered the English language. Even though she had quite a fear of water, Frances crossed the ocean thirty-seven times. At the time of her death more than 1,100 sisters had joined her order. Humility exists not as a timid weakness. Quite the opposite—for a Christian, humility embodies the virtue that allows the biggest accomplishments to occur through the most insignificant of people. It is this fact that ought to give us confidence in sharing our faith. If the Lord can use a sickly immigrant to bring about so many conversions, then he can use us to reach our family, friends, and community.

It seems commonplace in the history of the Church that those who humble themselves are raised to such high positions, but that is exactly how God shows the strength of his power. *St. Lawrence Giustiniani* (1381–1455) lived a true witness of what Jesus taught: "the last will be first, and the first last" (Mt 20:16). Lawrence hailed from a powerful, wealthy Venetian family. Disagreeing with his mother's secular plans, Lawrence joined the Augustinian Order of St. George in Alga, Italy. This period in history gave birth to the Protestant Reformation. Lawrence's order represented a microcosm of the Church at large at that time. Corruption, uneducated priests, and clergy living in excess afflicted their once simple, devout order. While he managed to escape the positions of power with his family, within a few years of his ordination Lawrence was elected as the General Superior of the order. His reforms proved to be so complete that he is referred to as the order's second founder. His humility still drove him to disregard his rank, and he would travel door to door begging for food. He established fifteen monasteries in his lifetime, and while he tried to avoid positions, Pope Nicholas V appointed Lawrence the first patriarch of Venice.

A close friend from Lawrence's youth heard about the religious life he had chosen. The nobleman was certain that being a religious was an incredible waste of Lawrence's life and talents. The friend laid into Lawrence about the terrible life decision he had made and berated him with insults. The saint lovingly listened and answered him with humility. Lawrence's longtime friend was so confounded that he changed his heart and joined the order at St. George's. Many times the desire to win an argument or prove that we are right accomplishes nothing. We are to be missionary disciples winning souls, not winning debates. Humility conquers pride. Humility can conquer us and perhaps those around us.

While some saints found their sanctity serving and evangelizing in active ways, others were called to a quieter way of life. Even a recluse monk like **St. Hospitius** (d. 581) can teach us about the work of evangelization. While little is known about the birth of Hospitius or his childhood, as an adult he left Egypt for the region of Gaul. There he found an abandoned, dilapidated tower near Cap Ferrat. Living as an isolated hermit, he practiced a strict life of asceticism. Hospitius kept a perpetual Lenten fast. He wore heavy chains to remind himself of his sin. Reputation of his holiness spread, and people began to seek out Hospitius for his wisdom and counsel. Hospitius worked miracles and warned people of a coming attack from the Lombards.

In 575, the Lombards conquered Gaul. The soldiers entered Hospitius's tower. With one look at the thin man in chains, they took him to be a criminal. "Yes! In the eyes of God, I am a criminal," Hospitius proclaimed. "I am a great sinner." A soldier raised his sword to strike the "criminal" dead.

However, the soldier's arm stiffened like concrete and could not be moved. When Hospitius made the sign of the cross over the paralyzed arm, the soldier was free. After learning of Hospitius's God, the soldier converted and became a monk. The soldier later in life met St. Gregory of Tours, who passed down to us this story.

The humility of Hospitius allowed God to do what only God could do—defend him. Many times our pride interferes in the work of evangelization. We presume to know what God needs to do in this given moment instead of submitting to his will. We must remember that evangelization is not *our* work but *his* work. Pope Francis wrote, "One who believes may not be presumptuous; on the contrary, truth leads to humility, since believers know that, rather than ourselves possessing truth, it is truth which embraces and possesses us."[38] We do not own the Gospel, but as disciples we belong to it, and as missionaries we are its ambassadors. In humility Hospitius was willing to die a martyr, but God had other plans. In our dealings with family and friends, can we lay our plans down to allow our Lord to work?

God's providence has a beautiful way of bringing about the kinds of saints the Church needs at exactly that point in time. *Pope St. Pius V* (1504–1572) was a leader that the Church needed at one of the most difficult times in history. He became pope in 1566, in the midst of the Protestant Reformation and just after the conclusion of the Council of Trent. Western civilization was being attacked by the Turks of the Ottoman Empire. Europeans were not free to sail on the Mediterranean Sea or visit the Holy Lands. The Church herself desperately needed great reform. Pius V proved to be the pope who could lead the way.

While Pius assumed the duties of pope for only six years, he accomplished a lifetime of work. He published the Church's first universal catechism, referred to as the Roman Catechism or the Catechism of the Council of Trent. Pius revised the Liturgy of the Hours and the Roman Missal, which remained untouched until the twentieth century. To help shine a light on how the reforms should look, Pius declared St. Thomas Aquinas to be a Doctor of the Church. But perhaps Pius's greatest historical accomplishment was during the Battle of Lepanto in 1571. The Turkish fleet was sweeping the Mediterranean Sea and threatening mainland Europe. Pope Pius managed to arrange an alliance between Spain and Italy known as the Holy League. As the confrontation approached, Pius implored all Catholics to pray a Rosary to the Mother of God. On October 7, the churches of Europe were filled with the faithful praying; miraculously, the greatly outnumbered Holy League decisively defeated the Turkish navy in the battle. The Church celebrates October 7 as the Feast of Our Lady of the Rosary still today.

While Pope Pius did everything in his political power to save Europe, ultimately he humbly relied not on his strength but on the Blessed Mother's intercession. Humility was at the core of his life. When Pius became pope, he continued to wear his coarse Dominican habit underneath the plush papal garments. An English nobleman, a Protestant, visited the Vatican and witnessed Pope Pius V kissing the feet of a beggar. The Englishman converted to Catholicism. With humility like that of Pius, our battles can be won even today. Whether we win over a single heart with a single humble act or change history by relying on the providence of God, we can rest assured that humility has the strength to change the world.

We all struggle with the sin of pride—some, like myself, more than others. I am fearful in thinking of how many times my pride has interfered with God using me to spread the Gospel. But that does not stop me from pursuing this most precious treasure of humility; in fact, it inspires me to pray for it daily. We should take heart in Pope Francis's words: "If we are to understand, forgive and serve others from the heart, our pride has to be healed and our humility must increase."[39] Our humility must grow to the point where we disappear in the eyes and ears of those who meet us, and they only see and hear Christ.

ST. PIO OF PIETRELCINA

ST. GREGORY
NAZIANZUS

ST. MARIA
GORETTI

ST. JOHN GUALBERT

Characteristic 3

MERCIFUL

The Church feels the urgent need to proclaim God's mercy. Her life is authentic and credible only when she becomes a convincing herald of mercy. She knows that her primary task, especially at a moment full of great hopes and signs of contradiction, is to introduce everyone to the great mystery of God's mercy by contemplating the face of Christ. The Church is called above all to be a credible witness to mercy, professing it and living it as the core of the revelation of Jesus Christ.

— Pope Francis [40]

Pope Francis has referred to the Church as a "field hospital." [41] What a profound image! A field hospital is a temporary hospital established near a war zone or place of crisis to give immediate medical attention to the wounded. This powerful description of the mission of the Church leaves a lasting impression. Whether we like it or not, we are already in the battle zone for souls. The war rages all around us, in our communities, workplaces, and homes. Wounded souls lay in wait. Some wounds penetrate very deeply, and some lie just below the surface; some show visibly, and some hide behind walls. But everyone is wounded and longing for the healing mercy of God. We are called to administer the mercy to those around us:

> Mercy is the very foundation of the Church's life. All of her pastoral activity should be caught up in the tenderness she makes present to believers; nothing in her preaching and in her witness to the world can be lacking in mercy. The Church's very credibility is seen in how she shows merciful and compassionate love. The Church "has an endless desire to show mercy." ... The time has come for the Church to take up the joyful call to mercy once more. It is time to return to the basics and to bear the weaknesses and struggles of our brothers and sisters. Mercy is the force that reawakens us to new life and instils in us the courage to look to the future with hope.[42]

The Church does everything to bring humanity to God's mercy — and saints, in a very real sense, could be called "Agents of Mercy." They intensely understand their own need for the mercy of God. This understanding leads to joy, gratitude, and a great boldness to offer and share mercy with everyone they encounter.

St. Pio of Pietrelcina (1887–1968) died before I was born. But I was keenly aware of his life, because growing up in Catholic schools, I constantly heard stories of the mystical Padre Pio. Born as Francesco Forgione, he took the name Pio, after Pope Pius I, when he entered the Capuchin order at Morcone at the young age of fifteen. Even though Pio struggled with health issues, he was ordained in 1910 to the priesthood. Everything changed for Padre Pio on September 20, 1918, when he received the wounds of Christ on his hands and feet known as the stigmata. Throughout his life the wounds were studied by doctors, but no medical explanation could be provided. To the faithful, the sacred wounds on Pio's body testified to his personal holiness. Pilgrims from all over the world flocked to him. Miraculous stories surrounded Padre Pio. Reports of physical healings, reading of souls, the scent of roses around him, prophesy, and even bilocation (physically being in two locations at the same time) brought even more attention and criticism. But Padre Pio bore the accusations as he bore the stigmata, with quiet suffering and offering it all for the salvation of souls.

A man wrapped up in the criminal underworld wanted to marry a different woman. In the early 1920s divorce was not the norm, so he hatched a perfect plan to murder his wife. This evil plan included taking his devout wife to meet Padre Pio, whom she admired. The husband planned his alibi and would murder her in the field as she returned from the friary. First the man went to the friary to schedule a time for his wife to meet with Padre Pio. However, while he was there he felt an overwhelming compulsion to go into the confessional. As he knelt and began to make the Sign of the Cross, Padre Pio from the other side began to yell, "Go away! Go away! Don't you know that it is forbidden to kill somebody?" The saintly priest came out of his confessional and shooed the man away. As the would-be murderer made his retreat, he fell into the mud face first and, in a moment of grace, repented of his sin. He returned, begging Padre Pio to hear his confession. With great gentleness and mercy Padre Pio heard the confession. At the same time he recited for the man his past sins, even the details of the planned murder. Padre Pio further predicted that if he returned to his wife, loved her, and obeyed the word of God, that they would be blessed with a child. The following year the man returned to Padre Pio completely converted and with his wife and child.

No sin exists that is too big for God's mercy to triumphantly forgive. There are no sins that the blood of Jesus cannot wash. As this man learned, not even a life of crime and premeditated murder could stop the love of God from making a new life. If a person sincerely and humbly repents, the Lord of the Universe is ready to forgive. "God never tires of forgiving us," said Pope Francis, "we are the ones who tire of seeking his mercy."[43] We must constantly remind ourselves of this message. It is also the core message of the work of evangelization. We must proclaim it loud and clear.

In my informal survey by attending dozens of confirmations, I believe that **St. Maria Goretti** (1890–1902) must be the most chosen confirmation name for girls, and for good reason. She stands as the saint of young people, of purity, and a premier example of mercy. Maria grew up in a poor farming family. When her father died, she was left to raise her siblings while her mother worked the fields. A twenty-year-old neighbor boy, Alessandro Serenelli, took an impure interest in Maria. She refused his advances and encouraged him to repent. With his futile attempts frustrated and a heart full of anger, he attacked Maria on July 5, 1902. Maria, much smaller in stature, fended him off as best she could. While Alessandro was not able to rape her, he stabbed her fourteen times. Maria died the following day, but not before she said, "I forgive Alessandro Serenelli ... and I want him with me forever." Wow! What mercy! Maria is the youngest canonized saint. Her canonization ceremony in 1950 was so large that for the first time in history it was performed outside in St. Peter's Square.

The death of Maria marked not the end of this story of mercy, but rather just the beginning. Alessandro was immediately arrested. Because he was a minor, he avoided the death penalty or life imprisonment; instead, he was sentenced to thirty years in prison. Alessandro's anger only grew in prison, forcing them to put him in solitary confinement. In one incident he attacked a visiting priest. But six years into his sentence, Maria appeared to Alessandro in a dream. In the dream Maria gave Alessandro the gift of fourteen lilies. By the grace of God, Alessandro accepted this gift of mercy and changed his life.

Alessandro became such a model prisoner that he was released three years early. One of the first acts Alessandro did when he was released was to seek out Maria's mother to ask for forgiveness, which she gave promptly. In 1937 Alessandro joined the Capuchin Franciscans as a lay brother, where he grew in peace and holiness until his death in 1970. So complete was his conversion that today there is a case open for the canonization of Alessandro Serenelli! Maria Goretti was such a vessel of the Lord's mercy that it not only made her a saint, but it also may have made another saint. That is our goal for the work of evangelization—to make saints through making known the mercy of the Lord.

If you feel that things never go your way and your own life is not in your hands, then *St. Gregory Nazianzus* (ca. 329–390) is the saint for you. While Gregory sought the quiet life of a monk, he was ordained against his will. Later, again against his wishes, Gregory was appointed a bishop by his longtime friend, St. Basil the Great. No matter how much he detested the political battles of this time, he was unable to avoid them. During the fourth century, political peace intertwined with peace within the Church, and the Arian heresy stood as a threat to both. Gregory fought fiercely against Arianism both in his peaching and writings, which earned him the title of Doctor of the Church. In the early Church, only two people are referred to simply as "The Theologian." One is St. John the Evangelist, who wrote the fourth Gospel, and the other is Gregory Nazianzus.

Gregory was appointed patriarch of Constantinople, and his battle against the Arian heresy was so successful that he became one of its greatest threats. Gregory's enemies viciously attacked his teaching and character. When those tactics proved unsuccessful, they came to their final conclusion that Gregory must be killed. The Arians hired a young man to fulfill the job. The assassin was unable to follow through with his duties once he looked Gregory in the eyes. He immediately confessed and repented to the saint. Without hesitation Gregory forgave his assailant, and they become friends. Not only did the heretics fail in their endeavor, but to the citizens of Constantinople, the saint's holiness was confirmed.

How different would our families or workplaces be if we were always the first to forgive? How different would it be if we showed mercy by forgiving even when it was not requested? These are not optional for us if we say we are Christians, as Pope Francis teaches us:

> Jesus affirms that mercy is not only an action of the Father, it becomes a criterion for ascertaining who his true children are. In short, we are called to show mercy because mercy has first been shown to us. Pardoning offenses becomes the clearest expression of merciful love, and for us Christians it is an imperative from which we cannot excuse ourselves. At times how hard it seems to forgive! And yet pardon is the instrument placed into our fragile hands to attain serenity of heart. To let go of anger, wrath, violence, and revenge are necessary conditions to living joyfully.[44]

To be the ambassadors of mercy we must be rich in mercy like our Heavenly Father. This can only occur if we are fully aware of the mercy we have received, and thus realize we cannot withhold that same gracious act from those around us.

There have been many movies based on the drama of avenging a family member's death. That was reality for **St. John Gualbert** (ca. 990–1073). John was born to a Florentine family of high class and wealth. For reasons that are not clear, John's only brother, Hugo, was murdered. John's father swore vengeance on the perpetrator and made his remaining son vow the same promise. The moment finally arrived on a Good Friday. John had the murderer trapped on a street with no escape. He drew his sword to fulfill his father's wish. The murderer fell to the ground and begged for mercy — and he called upon the passion and death of Jesus to spare his life. Taken aback, John paused, lifted the man up, embraced him, and announced that in the name of Jesus he would forgive.

John proceeded immediately to a church. He prayed for forgiveness and received a miraculous sign that the Lord had granted his request. A few years later he founded a religious order strictly observing the Rule of St. Benedict, called the Order of Vallombrosa. By the time of his death he had founded twelve monasteries—all because he let go of vengeance and offered mercy.

How many grudges are we holding on to right now? Whether grudges are over small or large matters, they will remain obstacles to the work of evangelization. It will be difficult to be instruments of the mercy of Jesus Christ to anyone if we are not willing to forgive as well. Once we can forgive, quickly and readily, an amazing thing occurs—we are set free! The freedom of forgiveness grants us the ability to accomplish all that is God's will. Showing mercy like John is the path that will save our souls and the many souls the Lord is going to bring into our path.

Mercy lies at the heart of the Gospel. It lies at the heart of being a Christian. While those outside of Catholicism find it awkward that we have crucifixes in our churches and homes, for us it is the sign of mercy. Pope Francis wants us to remember this often:

We need constantly to contemplate the mystery of mercy. It is a wellspring of joy, serenity, and peace. Our salvation depends on it. Mercy: the word reveals the very mystery of the Most Holy Trinity. Mercy: the ultimate and supreme act by which God comes to meet us. Mercy: the fundamental law that dwells in the heart of every person who looks sincerely into the eyes of his brothers and sisters on the path of life. Mercy: the bridge that connects God and man, opening our hearts to the hope of being loved forever despite our sinfulness.[45]

The saints were such effective evangelists of mercy because they knew and appreciated their own great need for mercy. The more we are aware of the greatness of the mercy our Lord offers us, the more our desire will be to speak of that mercy. The more we can forgive those who hurt us, the more credible our testimony of mercy will be to the lost.

ST. ELIZABETH OF PORTUGAL

ST. LEO I

ST. FRANCES
OF ROME

ST. CLEMENT HOFBAUER

Characteristic 4

PEACEFUL

We must never forget that we are pilgrims journeying alongside one another. This means that we must have sincere trust in our fellow pilgrims, putting aside all suspicion or mistrust, and turn our gaze to what we are all seeking: the radiant peace of God's face. Trusting others is an art and peace is an art. Jesus told us: "Blessed are the peacemakers" (Mt 5:9). In taking up this task, also among ourselves, we fulfil the ancient prophecy: "They shall beat their swords into ploughshares" (Is 2:4).

— Pope Francis [46]

A key characteristic of Christ's mission clearly evident in Scripture is the establishment of peace, "I have said this to you, that in me you may have peace. In the world you have tribulation; but be of good cheer, I have overcome the world" (Jn 16:33). When Christ greeted his apostles for the first time after his death and resurrection, he proclaimed, "Peace be with you" (Jn 20:19, 21). Furthermore, when he sent his disciples out to announce the coming of the kingdom, they were to do so with the greeting, "Peace be to this house!" (Lk 10:5).

However, the peace of Christ is very different from the world's understanding of peace (cf. Jn 14:27). Christian peace, a fruit of the Holy Spirit, first grows in the human heart. It implies not simply an interior peace, but also peace with our neighbor. We need only to think of the Beatitudes: "Blessed are the peacemakers, for they shall be called sons of God" (Mt 5:9). Pope Francis makes the connection between this beatitude and the work of evangelization: "By preaching Jesus Christ, who is himself peace (cf. Eph 2:14), the new evangelization calls on every baptized person to be a peacemaker and a credible witness to a reconciled life."[47] The apostle James also makes the same connection: "And the harvest of righteousness is sown in peace by those who make peace" (Jas 3:18). The saints of the Church were producers of a great "harvest of righteousness" because peace was so prevalent in their hearts. Whether it was during drama in their families or times of war, the saints demonstrate how to be peacemakers.

St. Elizabeth of Portugal (1271–1336) influenced others toward peace from the moment she was born. It was on that day that her father and grandfather reconciled after a long family feud. "The Peacemaker" was named after another saint we have discussed, her great-aunt St. Elizabeth of Hungary. Similar to her great-aunt, Elizabeth was pious from childhood. She married King Denis of Portugal at a very young age. He was a good ruler and shrewd politician, but the exact opposite as a husband and Christian. Denis became abusive, detached, and unfaithful to Elizabeth. She constantly sought and prayed for his conversion, only showing him gentleness, respect, and unconditional love. Elizabeth raised her two children and seven others from Denis's extramarital affairs. Moreover, she loved them as if they were her own.

King Denis and Elizabeth's oldest son was Alfonso. When Alfonso came of age, he resented his father's favoritism toward his illegitimate sons. The heated rivalry between father and son escalated to the point of gathering armies. As the two armies readied for war, Elizabeth rode out into the middle of the battlefield and brought about a peaceful reconciliation. Her knack for fostering peace proved to be useful for Denis several more times and continued when Alfonso became the rightful king.

In 1324, Denis became deathly ill and bedridden. Despite the unfaithfulness of her husband, Elizabeth faithfully cared for him. Over the next year she rarely left his side, except to attend to her spiritual commitments in church. Her patience and prayerfulness were rewarded when Denis repented of his sinful life before his death in 1325, reconciled to God, and died in the good graces of the Church and his bride. Elizabeth was able to be a peacemaker because she knew the Prince of Peace so intimately. She lived such an authentic spiritual life that others were captivated by the peace she embodied. We can become attached to the anxieties, fears, rivalries, and jealousies of this world, but we can overcome them with the peace of Christ, which surpasses all understanding.

In the history of the Church, a few sainted popes have received the title "Great." The first to receive such a title was *Pope St. Leo I* (ca. 400–461). Leo the Great is also recognized as a Doctor of the Church. He reigned as pope for twenty-one years, during a time in history when Roman civilization and Western culture neared extinction. Leo did much to establish the role of the pope as a leading figure in the universal Church. During the Second Council of Ephesus in 449, Leo sent delegates with a statement of belief now referred to the "Tome of Leo." When it was read at the council, the bishops declared, "Peter has spoken through the mouth of Leo." Equal to Leo's influence on spiritual matters was his political role, which did much to try to save Western civilization.

History provides us with people who accomplished inspiring feats and with people who caused utter terror. Attila the Hun, who ruled central and eastern Europe during his life,

earned the nickname "The Scourge of God." Attila was a bru-
tal enemy and constant threat to what was left of the Eastern
and Western Roman Empires. He marched through northern
Italy and in 452 found himself at the gates of Rome. The Holy
Father stood guard of the Eternal City and decided he would
meet with the barbarian aggressor. Leo traveled from the safety of the city and entered the camp to speak directly to Attila.
There are no reliable records of what was spoken in this his-
toric conversation, but the outcome is certain: Attila left. The
Huns reported later that Attila jokingly said he could defeat
any man but not the Lion (Leo is Latin for "lion").

The interaction with Attila was not just beginner's luck.
In 455 the Vandals arrived at the doorstep of Rome. While Leo
did not dissuade them from entering the city, he did manage
to convince the Vandals to refrain from burning and destroy-
ing Rome.

In doing the work of evangelization, we are going to
encounter moments of crisis. Moments will come in which it
will seem like the next action will bring down everything we
have worked for. Like Pope Leo, we must walk into the storm
with bold courage, secure in the knowledge that peace resides
within our hearts and that it is God's will to secure peace in
our families and relationships with others.

Bringing the Gospel to family can indeed be very challenging. We can look to *St. Frances of Rome* (1384–1440) for
an example of a peaceful witness of Christian charity amongst
family members who disliked her. Frances was raised in a
wealthy family and at a young age desired nothing more than
to become a religious. Her parents, though, had different plans.
They arranged her marriage to the extremely wealthy Lorenzo
Ponziano, the commander of the papal army. He was a good
man who loved Frances and her virtues, even encouraging her
to continue her works of mercy. Not only was Frances young

and pious, but she was extremely shy. Her mother-in-law, Cecilia, expected a young woman of such respectable background to be entertaining guests and visiting other aristocrats in the city. However, Frances preferred fasting to feasting with the wealthy. Cecilia was cruel to Frances, and her in-law problems got worse before getting better.

After Lorenzo was injured in a battle, he retired to his home and was compassionately attended to by his saintly wife. Lorenzo desired to see their son Battista married before he might die, so they found a young and beautiful bride, Mobilia. Unfortunately, she had a fiery temper, and Frances was usually the target of her wrath. Mobilia would slander Frances both to Battista and even in public. In the middle of a tirade against her mother-in-law, Mobilia was struck by a deadly illness. Frances peacefully cared for her daughter-in-law. Overcome by the compassion, Mobilia repented of her sin and fell in love with her mother-in-law's kindness and gentleness. From that moment on she tried to model her life after that of Frances. No family is perfect. In every family there will be disagreements, misunderstandings, jealousy, and disappointments. Yet, if we can be the source of peace instead of the lightning rod, the Gospel of Christ will have a greater chance of transforming our loved ones. Frances did not try to win every argument or make sure her point was understood. Instead she allowed the peace of Christ that was within her to fill her house with authentic love.

Known as the second founder of the Redemptorists and the Apostle of Vienna, *St. Clement Hofbauer* (1751–1820) was a great evangelist in Poland and Austria. He was born to a poor peasant family in the present-day Czech Republic. After the death of his father when he was six, Clement set aside his desire to become a priest and instead entered a baker apprenticeship. By chance he became a baker in a Norbertine Abbey, which at least allowed him to be around the spiritual life that ignited his heart.

Once after a morning Mass during a torrential downpour, Clement helped three wealthy sisters to secure their carriage and opened the doors for them. The grateful women offered Clement a ride. Knowing of his sincere piety, the older sister inquired why he had not become a priest. Clement humbly explained his financial state. The sisters promised that if that was the only obstacle, he should consider it removed, and they paid for his seminary education at the University of Vienna.

On one of his pilgrimages to Rome, Clement promised to attend Mass the following morning at the first church from which he heard bells. In the morning the bells of San Giuliano rang and called out to Clement. He was so impressed by the liturgy and prayer of the Redemptorists at the parish that he asked to join them immediately. Shortly after his ordination as a Redemptorist priest, he was sent back to his home region of Poland and Austria. Those who knew Clement as a priest testified to the supernatural peace surrounding him. One of significant needs of the war-torn area was an orphanage. To raise funds for the orphans, Clement would beg. Bars at the time also provided gambling, which in Clement's mind made it a good opportunity for the patrons to grow in almsgiving as well. Once when Clement asked a man in a bar for alms, the man spat beer in his face. "That was for me," Clement responded. "Now what do you have for my boys." All of the patrons, including the spitter, were so moved by Clement's Christlike peaceful response that he left the bar with more than one hundred silver coins. In life people will say or do things to get underneath our skin. In these moments there could be more on the line than just a heated argument. Our reaction, if answered in the peace of Christ, could be what draws them into a new awareness of the love of God.

We live in a highly emotionally charged culture. Situations escalate quickly when our reactions are formed more by feelings rather than by rational thought. Our modes of communication such as email, texting, and social media allow for misunderstandings over the simplest expressions. As missionary disciples, we can use each of these situations to be peacemakers. But it is not our peace; it is his peace. "Peace I leave with you; my peace I give to you; not as the world gives do I give to you. Let not your hearts be troubled, neither let them be afraid" (Jn 14:27). So the next time someone is hurting at work, be bold: talk, listen, and console them. When a family member or friend makes a biting, passive-aggressive remark to you, respond in love as if they had complimented you. Allow the supernatural to overtake your natural reactions so that "the peace of God, which passes all understanding, will keep your hearts and your minds in Christ Jesus" (Phil 4:7), thus allowing others to know the same peace.

ST. THEODOSIUS
THE CENOBIARCH

ST. BRIGID OF
KILDARE

ST. RAYMOND
OF PENAFORT

ST. VENANTIUS

Characteristic 5

FAITHFUL

> It is the love of Christ that fills our hearts and impels us to evangelize…. Faith grows when it is lived as an experience of love received and when it is communicated as an experience of grace and joy. It makes us fruitful, because it expands our hearts in hope and enables us to bear life-giving witness: indeed, it opens the hearts and minds of those who listen to respond to the Lord's invitation to adhere to his word and become his disciples.
>
> — Pope Benedict XVI [48]

The work of evangelization accomplishes its goal when faith grows. More registered members of our parish or an increase in parish collections are only by-products of that goal. The goal is not to create "believers," for "even the demons believe—and shudder" (Jas 2:19). Through the power of the Holy Spirit, evangelization brings about faith-FULL disciples in authentic relationship with Jesus Christ. This authentic faith becomes life-changing. People cannot say they have come to faith and yet live a life the same as it was yesterday. Faith produces holiness, which means to be set apart. That separation marks a Christian as "different" and demands a boldness in the work of faith, as Pope Benedict encouraged us:

Confessing with the lips indicates in turn that faith implies public testimony and commitment. A Christian may never think of belief as a private act. Faith is choosing to stand with the Lord so as to live with him. This "standing with him" points towards an understanding of the reasons for believing. Faith, precisely because it is a free act, also demands social responsibility for what one believes. The Church on the day of Pentecost demonstrates with utter clarity this public dimension of believing and proclaiming one's faith fearlessly to every person. It is the gift of the Holy Spirit that makes us fit for mission and strengthens our witness, making it frank and courageous.[49]

We must understand this conversion of heart to a life of faith if we are going to be effective evangelists. The saints were so effective in their work of evangelization because their walk of faith was so profound. The witness of the saints to the life-changing power of faith convinced and converted many hearts because their personal relationship with Christ was so real.

St. Theodosius the Cenobiarch (423–529) was a man illuminated by the light of faith. Originally from the country that would become Turkey today, Theodosius was inspired by the faith of Abraham to become a hermit. Reports of his holiness spread and began to attract followers. Theodosius determined where to build his monastery by carrying charcoal throughout the Holy Land. When the charcoal miraculously lit on its own at Cathismus, Theodosius placed incense on it and immediately began construction. According to tradition, this location also marked the cave where the three magi slept when they received the message to avoid returning to Herod (cf. Mt 2:12). Today Theodosius is buried in that same cave.

The early Church was plagued with misunderstandings about the nature of Jesus Christ. Theodosius battled the Eutychian heresy during his lifetime. Eutychianism incorrectly held that Jesus possessed only one nature, which was a mixture of divinity and humanity.[50] The Emperor Anastatius, influenced by the Eutychians, unfortunately sought peace in the Church by upholding the heresy. Anastatius sent Theodosius a bribe to accept the heresy. But he promptly distributed the money to the poor and continued teaching the orthodox Truth. In response, the emperor removed Theodosius from his position. In the face of the emperor's persecution, Theodosius traveled, imploring people to hold fast to the first four councils of the Church as if they were the four Gospels. His message emboldened the laity, and their zeal for the faith was manifested in widespread miracles.

If we are going to be effective evangelists, then our lives and lips must be mirrors of the teachings of the Church—all of them. As Catholics we give witness to the teaching that Jesus lived two thousand years ago. He suffered, died, and rose from the dead and continues to be physically present in the Eucharist—body, blood, soul, and divinity. These are extraordinary teachings that are difficult for the world to accept. However, how can we be convincing about such Truths if we do not hold to all the Church's teachings—even the controversial ones such as abortion, contraception, same-sex marriage, or medical ethics? Theodosius could have justified acceptance of the Eutychian heresy by telling himself that he believed in 98 percent of the teachings of the Church ... just not one in particular. His witness would have lacked the authentic integrity needed to rouse a passionate faith in people that could withstand persecution.

Many times the circumstances surrounding us are not conducive to evangelization. ***St. Raymond of Penafort*** (1175–1275) brought about deep conversions in difficult situations. Raymond had family ties to Spanish nobility, but the

Lord had plans for his intellectual and teaching skills other than mere politics. Perhaps because of his developed gift for teaching, Raymond eventually joined the Dominicans at the age of forty-seven. He had a passionate desire for the conversion of Jews and Muslims. Well before the time of modern ecumenical dialogue, Raymond held a public debate between a leading Jewish scholar and a Catholic convert from Judaism. It was Raymond who convinced St. Thomas Aquinas to write the famous *Summa Contra Gentiles*, one of Aquinas's greatest apologetical works. Along with King James of Aragon and St. Peter Nolasco, Raymond founded the Order of Our Lady of Ransom, which dedicated itself to rescuing Christians enslaved by Muslims.

King James enlisted the help of Raymond on a trip to the island of Majorca to assist in the conversion of Muslims. Though the king was goodhearted, he was not perfect and secretly brought a mistress along for the trip. When Raymond uncovered the secret, he demanded that the king send the scandalous woman away. James initially promised but failed to follow through on the request. The saint insisted that he would return to Spain if his request was not respected. But the king refused and threatened to punish anyone who assisted Raymond. In an incredible act of faith, Raymond hastened to the seashore, removed his black Dominican cloak and placed it on top of the water. He attached his walking stick to the cloak and stepped onto his "boat." Raymond sailed the 160 miles back to Spain in six hours. King James was so awestruck that he repented of his sin and subjected himself to the spiritual direction of Raymond to lead a devout life.

Faithfulness requires boldness and fortitude. At their core all long for Jesus Christ, whether they are aware of it or not. Raymond overcame any trace of fear of losing his position or friendship with the king in order to save him from sin. Are we willing to do the same? Can we overcome the fear of being considered an outcast at work? Can we overcome the fear of family or friends becoming angry at us if we share our faith? Are we prepared to handle the backlash on our social media networks if we state the clear teachings of the Church? If we can do this, like Raymond, our faith will be rewarded with the miraculous changing of hearts.

For the Irish there is one saint who comes closest to matching the fame of St. Patrick, and that is *St. Brigid of Kildare* (ca. 450–523). Her father was a pagan Druid chieftain, and her mother was a Christian slave. Tradition holds that she heard St. Patrick preach, which inspired her entire life. At eighteen she left her family and the idea of marriage to help the poor. Building up a following of like-minded women, she founded a monastery at Kildare. When Brigid needed land, she requested it from the pagan king. He laughed at the petition and generously offered her all the land her cloak could cover. Promptly Brigid removed her cloak and placed it on the ground. Her companions began to stretch out the cloak, which ended up covering twelve acres. The king not only gave her the land, money, and food, but he also became Christian.

Once a Druid chieftain who lived close to the monastery of Kildare was near death. Brigid was summoned by Christians who served in the chieftain's house. In her usual compassionate manner, Brigid consoled the dying man. At that time, straw on the ground of homes was commonplace; Brigid picked up some of the straw from the ground and fashioned it a cross, prompting the man to inquire what she was doing. Brigid spoke about the mystery of the cross and the love of her Savior, Jesus Christ. The pagan man, touched by her faith, was baptized shortly before his death.

Brigid was an effective evangelist because of her knowledge of the faith *and* her knowledge of the pagan

Druid religions. Not only was her father a Druid, but she was named after the goddess of fire. Her monastery was built underneath a magnificent oak tree, hence the name Kildare, "Church of the Oak." An oak tree had a sacred significance to the Druids. Also present at Kildare was a sacred fire that had been perpetually burning. Brigid did not put out the flame but instead gave it a Christian significance. That fire remained constantly lit by the sisters until the thirteenth century. To effectively evangelize, we must be familiar with the world around us. Our faith is reasonable; we have reasons why we believe what we believe. With these reasons we can enter into a dialogue with today's culture. This should give us great confidence to share the Gospel.

The fruit of faithfulness is more faithfulness, as evident from the heroic story of **St. Venantius** (ca. 235–250). Records of the life of Venantius are difficult to authenticate. But legend hands down his story as that of a great martyr. When he was only fifteen or seventeen, Venantius was recognized as Christian and brought in front of a judge. After many attempts to get the teenager to recant his faith, the judge ordered him to be scourged, burnt with torches, and hung upside down over a fire to suffocate from the smoke. Venantius faced his torture with absolute zeal for his faith. The secretary of the judge, being so moved by Venantius's courage, extinguished the fire and released him (though Venantius eventually was beheaded). The secretary was baptized and eventually also became a martyr.

Faithfulness, especially in times of trial, can bring about great fruitfulness. We will always face suffering. Most of the time suffering presents itself as a minor annoyance, such as getting cut off in traffic or finding the copy machine jammed for the fourth time. But there are times when we face suffering that brings us to our breaking point. Either way, how we suffer can give testimony to the glory of our Redeemer. We must suffer differently. We must suffer in a manner that displays the life, love, and eternal hope that Christ desires to bestow. At every turn Venantius's suffering brought about conversions. Our attempts at evangelization will be fruitful if we faithfully offer up our sufferings like Jesus Christ for the salvation of souls.

Faith is such a tremendous gift from God. Gifts are meant to be given and received. If we have received the gift of faith, then we must give it away. The *Catechism of the Catholic Church* describes it beautifully:

> Faith is a personal act—the free response of the human person to the initiative of God who reveals himself. But faith is not an isolated act. No one can believe alone, just as no one can live alone. You have not given yourself faith as you have not given yourself life. The believer has received faith from others and should hand it on to others. Our love for Jesus and for our neighbor impels us to speak to others about our faith. Each believer is thus a link in the great chain of believers. I cannot believe without being carried by the faith of others, and by my faith I help support others in the faith. (CCC 166)

Someone helped us receive the gift of faith. For many of us it was our parents, but perhaps it was a spouse or friend. The *Catechism* offers a subtle challenge: How are we the "link" for helping someone to receive the faith?

Characteristic 6

HOPEFUL

"In the desert we rediscover the value of what is essential for living; thus in today's world there are innumerable signs, often expressed implicitly or negatively, of the thirst for God, for the ultimate meaning of life. And in the desert people of faith are needed who, by the example of their own lives, point out the way to the Promised Land and keep hope alive." In these situations we are called to be living sources of water from which others can drink. At times, this becomes a heavy cross, but it was from the cross, from his pierced side, that our Lord gave himself to us as a source of living water. Let us not allow ourselves to be robbed of hope!

— Pope Francis [51]

Throughout history hope has served as one of the most powerful factors in generating monumental change. Hope inspires us to accomplish more than we would think possible, and it keeps us from falling into despair when faced with daunting circumstances. For Christians, because it is a supernatural theological virtue, hope carries with it an eternal dimension beyond what this life can offer. In this way hope speaks to every human heart, because eternal life with God is exactly what all of us are longing for whether we are aware of it or not. God would not place that desire for eternal life in us unless he was willing to bring us there.

The saints lead the way as our shining examples of hope. They let us know that God can turn sinners into saints. They witness to the fact that we are made for more than this world has to offer and that the promises of Christ are true. What our brothers and sisters in heaven are to us, so we must be to this world dimmed by hopelessness (cf. Eph 4:11–13). The saints did not simply have hope; they also *lived* hope, *performed* hope. By our living authentic hope, those around us will be inspired to the hope that, as St. Paul promises, "does not disappoint" (Rom 5:5).

For many, the art of evangelizing family members is difficult, yet **St. Clotilde** (474–545) gives us hope that it can be done. Clotilde was the daughter of a Catholic Burgundian king. Her uncle was an Arian and usurped the crown by killing Clotilde's father, mother, and brothers. Because of her beauty and virtue, her uncle kept Clotilde alive.

Clovis of the Franks asked for Clotilde's hand in marriage to further his political ambitions. She agreed to marry the king once he promised to respect her and allow her to live her Catholic faith in peace. As soon as they were married, Clotilde sought her husband's conversion. She was careful to compliment her husband's virtues and meek to counter his temper. She won his heart by involving herself in his interests. Clotilde laughed at the humor and games Clovis found funny. But even then Clovis would not convert for fear of losing his followers. In 496, King Clovis was losing in the Battle of Tolbiac. He prayed to the "God of Clotilde" for assistance and promised he would receive baptism if he gained the victory. Clovis won the battle. So he was baptized that Christmas Eve by St. Remigius. Along with his conversion came the rest of the Franks, and France is still referred as the Church's Eldest Daughter.

Because of his newfound hope and at the request of Clotilde, Clovis built a beautiful church in Paris, which today is called St. Genevieve.

In my travels I have met many parents and grandparents who are near despair thinking of the faith of their children and grandchildren. But even in the most grievous of situations, there is always hope. As much as we desire for our family members or loved ones to return to the Church, we can be certain that our Lord wants it more. Clotilde did not nag or pressure Clovis. She prayed for the wisdom and strength to be what Christ needed her to be for him. That must be our role as effective evangelists for our family and loved ones. All our hope for them resides in the promises of Christ, and not us. That is precisely the way the hope we have for our family is real and certain.

In the work of evangelization, it does not take long to feel the enemy at our heels, but *St. Germanus of Auxerre* (ca. 378–448) demonstrated that hope overcomes even the greatest odds. Germanus was a successful, well-educated nobleman. After becoming the governor of Auxerre, he became worldly despite his Christian roots. To show off his skill at hunting, Germanus would hang the trophies of the hunt on a tree that the local pagans believed was sacred. St. Amator scolded Germanus, insisting that the trophies could lead Christians to revert back to their pagan ways. Germanus refused, so Amator cut down the tree and burned the prized trophies. Germanus grew so livid that he hunted down the holy man with murderous intentions. While a detailed description of their encounter does not exist, we do know that there was a complete reversal of fates. Miraculously, Amator walked away alive, and Germanus walked away ordained. He took the bizarre turn of fortunes as a sign from God, turned his life around, and shortly afterward succeeded Amator as the bishop of Auxerre.

As a bishop, Germanus was sent on a mission to Britain to counter the heresy that had taken strong root in the country. While he was there, the territory was invaded by a band of Saxons on raiding excursions. The bishop took the matter in his own hands. Leading a greatly outnumbered troop of soldiers, he ordered them to light fires and on his command shout out "Alleluia! Alleluia! Alleluia!" The sound was so loud that the invading Saxons dropped their weapons and ran. Many of the British troops converted, becoming Christians that Easter. An important lesson is learned here—numbers will not always be in our favor, but we have a certain hope that the victory is already won. We will encounter uphill battles against problems that seem much larger than we are. Like Germanus, all we can do is to count on the name of our Lord, for he is our sure refuge, strength, and hope.

Often in the Gospel we see Jesus spending time with people on the fringe of society, like the Samaritan woman and sinners. **St. John Francis Regis** (1597–1640) would also spend his ministry in the same way. Educated by Jesuits, John entered the Society of Jesus when he was eighteen. He proved himself to be very talented intellectually, but where John excelled most was in his desire for saving souls. His zeal and attention were for the hopeless, the marginalized of society. As he would often say, "The rich never lack confessors." John desired to follow in the footsteps of the Jesuit St. Isaac Jogues by being a missionary in Canada, but instead he was sent to the rural communities of France.

Traveling the back roads of France, John worked with the poor, prisoners, farmers, French Protestants, and the forgotten of society. He established safety houses for prostitutes, whom John called the "Daughters of Refuge." Some of the churches that he visited were so utterly abandoned that they had not had the sacraments celebrated in more than two decades. Because people were not in churches, John would preach in backyards, on porches, and even in bars. Traveling the French countryside was not easy in the seventeenth century. At one parish John was snowed in for three weeks. With very little food, no heat, and no bed except for the ground, he continued to preach. A parishioner said he would stand on a pile of snow to preach all day and then hear confessions all night. When the pastor returned, he remarked, "I just cannot recognize my parishioners," so complete was their conversion.

We must be honest and admit that evangelizing those who are like us—sound like us, look like us, and act like us—is more comfortable. However, to fail to bring the Gospel to the marginalized of society is a crime against the Gospel itself. Christ is the Savior of all humanity, and that includes the most hopeless person we will ever meet. Where would we be without faith in our lives right now? Would we not also be without hope? This awareness is what propels us forward in sharing what we have been given, as Pope Francis shares:

> All of us are called to offer others an explicit witness to the saving love of the Lord, who despite our imperfections offers us his closeness, his word and his strength, and gives meaning to our lives. In your heart you know that it is not the same to live without him; what you have come to realize, what has helped you to live and given you hope, is what you also need to communicate to others.[52]

St. John Francis Regis's life compels us to take a close look around our neighborhoods, schools, workplaces, and back alleys to see who it is that Jesus longs to love and bring a new hope to through us.

St. Vitalis of Gaza (d. 625) was an evangelist who did everything in his power to reach the lost and hopeless. Vitalis was a hermit living in the desert when he felt called to move to Alexandria, Egypt, for a new mission. When he arrived in Alexandria, he did two things. First, Vitalis gave up the life of a hermit to work instead as a manual day laborer. Second, he researched the name of every prostitute in the city. After backbreaking work all day, he would take his pay and head to a brothel. As a paying "client" Vitalis would enter the room with the woman. He encouraged the woman to close her eyes and fall asleep, while Vitalis would pray for her all night. As this occurred night after night, Vitalis formed relationships with the women. He would teach them about their dignity in Jesus Christ and that there was a better way of life.

Vitalis's nightly behavior began to cause scandal and controversy in the city. Obviously, he instructed the young women to never speak about his visits, because the brothel would not allow him to return. One night when Vitalis was leaving a brothel, a man struck him on the head. He managed to make it home, where he passed away. It was only at his funeral that the full light of Vitalis's accomplishments came to light. Hundreds of prostitutes showed up with testimonies of what the holy man had done for them. Many of them left their former profession to become faithful wives, and some even entered convents. There is no such thing as a hopeless sinner if we are willing to reach out to them with the love of the Gospel.

Everything that we have said about hope is good information; but if it only remains information, then we have missed the point. Pope Benedict XVI taught us that hope is a virtue that cannot remain simply "informative"—it must become "performative."[53] Our lives and the decisions we make are different because we live in Christ. Hope changes us, it changes everything it encounters, and it has the power to change the world. The hope that Christ gives us must move out from us to the world, Pope Benedict says: "We become capable of the great hope, and thus we become ministers of hope for others. Hope in a Christian sense is always hope for others as well. It is an active hope, in which we struggle to prevent things moving towards the 'perverse end.' It is an active hope also in the sense that we keep the world open to God. Only in this way does it continue to be a truly human hope."[54]

ST. THOMAS OF
VILLANOVA

ST. PETER
CLAVER

ST. FRANCIS
OF PAOLA

ST. MARGARET
OF SCOTLAND

Characteristic 7

CHARITABLE

To be evangelizers of souls, we need to develop a spiritual taste for being close to people's lives and to discover that this is itself a source of greater joy. Mission is at once a passion for Jesus and a passion for his people. When we stand before Jesus crucified, we see the depth of his love which exalts and sustains us, but at the same time, unless we are blind, we begin to realize that Jesus' gaze, burning with love, expands to embrace all his people. We realize once more that he wants to make use of us to draw closer to his beloved people. He takes us from the midst of his people and he sends us to his people; without this sense of belonging we cannot understand our deepest identity.

— Pope Francis [55]

Nothing else separates Christianity from all the world's religions more than the virtue of love. God desires a loving relationship, not simply obedient servitude. The Beloved Disciple described it with three words: "God is love" (1 Jn 4:16). Because of the Father's love, he sent his only begotten son so that we would know that love in a real and tangible manner (Jn 3:16). The concrete and potent love of God changes everything it encounters. This love is so powerful that it can bring something out of nothing. It can bring good out of evil. It can raise the dead to life, and it can turn sinners into saints. In fact this love becomes the clearest way to identify an authentic Christian: "A new commandment I give to you, that you love one another; even as I have loved you, that you also love one another. By this all men will know that you are my disciples, if you have love for one another" (Jn 13:34–35). Authentic love becomes the reason for evangelization. It is the method of, as well as the goal of, evangelization. The saints' love for their neighbors compelled them to evangelize. They first evangelized others by showing them their worth and dignity through acts of charity. Through the saints' love, their neighbors found the source of all love in Jesus Christ.

St. Thomas of Villanova (1488–1555) gave everything he had out of love. He was born in Spain to parents who instructed him in a life of complete charity. Thomas entered college at the age of fifteen. In a brief time he earned a degree and began teaching. He earned an excellent reputation as a professor. Thomas joined the Order of St. Augustine and made his religious vows on November 25, 1517. This was one month after another Augustinian monk named Martin Luther posted the "95 Theses" igniting the Protestant Reformation. He was elected provincial of the Augustinians where his leadership and evangelistic zeal could blossom. After denying several times the appointment as an archbishop, he finally accepted out of humble obedience. His desire for souls prompted him to send monks to Mexico and the Philippines. Thomas built a college specifically for Muslim converts. But he would be best known for his work with the poor.

So impressive was Thomas's charity and evangelization that the Holy Roman Emperor Charles V remarked that he had even converted the stones and had turned the city into a monastery. He served more than four hundred poor people every day from his residency. Thomas's plan was not to improve only the lives of the poor but also the spiritual lives of the wealthy. He encouraged those with wealth to be richer in mercy and charity than in worldly possessions. At his death, it was said that there were no poor left except the archbishop.

Thomas's compassion toward the poor was matched only by his love for sinners. There was a priest in the diocese who was not a good Christian let alone a good priest. Thomas on several occasions attempted to appeal to the priest's sense of decency, but to no avail. While the vice of the priest is unknown, it was severe enough that the archbishop had him placed in jail for eight days. Then the prisoner was brought to Thomas's home. The saint threw himself on the ground below a crucifix and cried for the priest's offenses. Overcome by the archbishop's love, the priest repented and claimed the sorrow to be his own. Love makes us keenly aware of how we offend those we love: our family, friends, spouse, and especially God. The more we love, the more repugnant sin becomes. We, like Thomas, should love sinners so much that they too will walk through sorrow to know love.

No other ministry in the history of the Church is more unique and successful than the work of **St. Peter Claver** (1580–1654). As a Spanish Jesuit who was reared to be a priest from his youth, Peter would have excelled at any mission. St. Alphonsus Rodriguez, Peter's mentor, convinced him that he should head to the New World. After the long voyage, Peter arrived at the port of Cartagena in present-day Columbia. This port served as a major hub for the slave trade, which had been established there for more than one hundred years. The black slaves arrived at Cartagena after a two-month voyage in some of the worst human conditions imaginable. The port received about one thousand slaves every single month. These slaves became the subject of Peter's love and compassion.

Peter demanded to be informed every time a slave ship came to port, no matter the time of day or night. He ran to the ships immediately upon arrival and would go to the lowest level of the boat where the slaves were kept. With a smile on his face, he would tend to the sick and try to calm their fears. Using interpreters, Peter was able to teach the slaves about Christ and his love for each of them. When the slaves were transported to markets, the saint would bring them bread, lemons, brandy, and tobacco. Many of the slaves experienced the saving love of Christ through Peter. The lowest estimates provided by historical records indicate that Peter baptized more than three hundred thousand people!

Most other missionaries working with the slaves never found the success that Peter experienced. Missionaries often baptized slaves without instruction, care, or love; thus the slaves many times despised their baptisms. One of the great popes for the New Evangelization, Pope Paul VI said, "Modern man listens more willingly to witnesses than to teachers, and if he does listen to teachers, it is because they are witnesses."[56] Peter embodied Pope Paul VI's teaching four hundred years before it was ever written. He exemplified a method of evangelization that is communicated with the hands before the lips. "Love is shown more in deeds than in words," said Peter. "Love does not mean that I like to do what I'm doing; love means that I do it." It is one thing to say that we love our neighbor, but in order for them to *know* we do, we must *show* them.

For a Catholic to be named after a saint is extremely common, but to live up to that saint name is exactly what **St. Francis of Paola** (1416–1507) extraordinarily accomplished. After a pilgrimage with his parents to Rome at the age of fifteen, Francis returned home resolving to live life as a hermit. This was no childish aspiration. He took up solo residency in a cave on his family's property. Francis's reputation as a holy man spread, and when he was nineteen, two men joined him. As more men joined Francis, he formed them into the Hermits of St. Francis. Later they became known as the Minim Friars, because they were committed to be the least in the kingdom. Word of miracles and prophesy spread throughout Italy and beyond. When King Louis XI of France was near death, he requested the presence of the saintly friar. Louis, who was known to lack any form of authentic piety, just wanted a miraculous healing. However, Francis insisted that the king should be more concerned about eternal life than extending his life. Louis died peacefully in the arms of the saint.

As Francis become more renowned, his contemporaries grew jealous. A monsignor in Rome preached against the stories of his life and miracles. When it seemed to have little effect on the saint, the monsignor made the decision to deliver his attack in person. Francis kindly welcomed the accuser and patiently listened to every accusation. After the list of reported allegations was aired, Francis walked over to the fire and, with his bare hands, grabbed some of the charcoal. He invited the monsignor to come close to the charcoal, saying he must be cold without the least warmth of charity. Upon witnessing the miracle, the monsignor returned to Rome and helped to have Francis's order canonically approved.

Depending on whom we are around, it can be all too easy to allow the embers of charity in our hearts to be extinguished. The world can be a dark and cynical place if we do not burn brightly with the fire of love. Those who knew Francis reported that he would often say a simple prayer: "Out of love." When he worked a miracle, received a compliment, met an obstacle, Francis would say, "Out of love." Our evangelization efforts must be wrapped in the same motivation. The next time you are considering sharing the Gospel, think, "Out of love." When someone says no to your invitation, "Out of love." When someone thanks you for bringing them back to the Church, "Out of love."

Charity not only changes the recipient, but as **St. Margaret of Scotland** (1045–1093) demonstrated, it transforms the giver as well. Margaret's noble family hailed from England but was forced to flee by ship to escape William the Conqueror. While Scotland was not their destination, that is where providence led them. Malcolm III, a Scottish king, provided care and protection for the family. He also fell in love with Margaret and married her. For Margaret it was not enough to win his heart; she wanted to win Malcolm for Christ.

Malcolm was a good representative of the country of Scotland at the time. He was a good man but lacked the culture, refinement, and manners of the more civilized England. Margaret was able to transform the king as she won him over. She taught him how to pray from the depths of his heart. Although he could not read, Malcolm would carefully handle and kiss the queen's spiritual books. Often he would "steal" them in order to have them embossed with silver, gold, and gems. Everything Margaret loved he loved, and her main love was for the poor. Before meals the king and queen would invite the poor into their dining hall. The doors would be closed, leaving the hosts alone with their guest. Malcolm and Margaret would wash the feet of the poor and feed them. It is recorded that Margaret would never eat a meal without first feeding at least nine orphans and twenty-four adults. These acts of self-giving changed the king. Malcolm became a strong, virtuous leader. At the prompting of his saintly wife, they built churches and monasteries all across the island.

Who else would have been able to reach the heart of King Malcolm with the love of Jesus other than Margaret? Who is the King Malcolm in your life? Who is it that God has placed in your life whom only you can reach? I am firmly convinced that there are people in this life who can only be transformed by you and your love for them. Love them with a supernatural, unconditional love and do not just win their heart but win them for Christ.

St. Paul teaches us that the greatest of the Theological Virtues is love (cf. 1 Cor 13:13). This is so because love binds us to God. God does not want just our servile obedience but instead desires a loving relationship. However, a loving relationship with the Lord is only authenticated by our love of neighbor. Pope Francis makes this connection:

> "'For the measure you give will be the measure you get back' (Lk 6:36–38). What these passages make clear is the absolute priority of 'going forth from ourselves towards our brothers and sisters' as one of the two great commandments which ground every moral norm and as the clearest sign for discerning spiritual growth in response to God's completely free gift. For this reason, 'the service of charity is also a constituent element of the Church's mission and an indispensable expression of her very being.' By her very nature the Church is missionary."[57]

Love has the power to change us, and through us love has the power to change even the most hardened of hearts. Today you can be love incarnate! Your love can be what sets someone free to accept Christ's love for all eternity. Be that love to the world!

Conclusion

Studying the lives of the saints can become a daunting challenge for us. We begin to harbor fears of failing to measure up. The process by which a saint is declared to be a saint is called canonization. The word "canon" means "rule" or "measure." So the canonization process determines whether a person's life measures up to a life of heroic virtue. But once saints are canonized, they in turn become the measuring sticks of our lives. How do we measure up? We might feel that "they are saints and I am not," therefore "I will never accomplish what they accomplished." Pope Francis addressed this concern when he tweeted to the world, "The saints were not superhuman. They were people who loved God in their hearts, and who shared this joy with others."[58] I am certain that if the saints were asked about their holiness or accomplishments, they would be the first to declare that God was working through them and that they were unworthy instruments.

Pope St. John Paul II, the patron saint of the New Evangelization, taught: "The call to mission derives, of its nature, from the call to holiness. A missionary is really such only if he commits himself to the way of holiness.... The *universal call to holiness* is closely linked to the *universal call to mission*. Every member of the faithful is called to holiness and to mission.... The Church's missionary spirituality is a journey toward holiness."[59] So if we are willing to do the work of evangelization, then we first must be committed to pursuing holiness. We must pray to be saints. We must strive to be saints.

Only our cooperation with the grace of God will make us saints. But I have discovered some practical tips that will help us on this journey. In my research I read nearly five hundred stories or biographies on saints. I discovered that a remarkable number of saints knew other saints. There are those saints who were married to one another, such as Sts. Isidore and Maria de la Cabeza or Bls. Luigi Beltrame Quattrocchi and Maria Corsini. Then there are those who are related to one another, such as Sts. Monica and Augustine or Sts. Benedict and Scholastica. Entire families became saints, such as Sts. Louis and Zelie Martin and their daughter St. Therese; Sts. Gregory the Elder and Nonna and their son St. Gregory Nazianzus; and Sts. Basil the Elder and Macrina and their sons Sts. Basil the Great and Gregory of Nyssa. In my research, I discovered more than one hundred saints who knew other saints! All of this is not counting those in Scripture nor those who were martyred together. This says to me that becoming a saint is easier accomplished with friends. The call to holiness is difficult enough in this world; we do not have to make that journey alone. We must surround ourselves with like-minded people, friends who are serious about getting to heaven and bringing as many souls with them as possible.

It has also become evident to me that *saints are saint makers.* Many saints influenced others who would also become recognized saints, such as St. Ambrose and St. Augustine, St. John Bosco and St. Dominic Savio, and St. Ignatius of Loyola and St. Francis Xavier. This does not count all the noncanonized "saints" who were influenced in monasteries and convents by saints like Benedict, Teresa of Avila, Jane Frances de Chantal, Francis of Assisi, or Bernard of Clairvaux. The saints are bright lights that shine in the hearts of their friends.

The Church today needs you to be a saint and a missionary disciple! In the darkest times of Church history, God raised up some of the most amazing saints. Our era has already been blessed with Pope St. John Paul the Great and St. Teresa of Calcutta, but I am certain this is just the tip of the iceberg for the saints who will be coming. If we wholeheartedly answer the universal call to holiness and the moral obligation to evangelize, then such an army will come forth that has not been seen since the disciples walked out of the Upper Room. This is not idle dreaming but precisely what Pope St. John Paul taught would happen. The New Evangelization will bring forth a new springtime of faith. So the Church needs you to be a saintly missionary disciple! Let us call upon all the saints to help us answer this challenge with a resolute boldness: All you holy men and women, saints of God ... pray for us!

Notes

1. Hans Urs von Balthasar, *You Crown the Year with Your Goodness: Sermons throughout the Liturgical Year* (San Francisco: Ignatius Press, 1989), 209.

2. Pope Francis, Apostolic Exhortation, *Evangelii Gaudium* (Nov. 24, 2013), 233.

3. Ibid., 263.

4. Chris Stewart and Tony Brandt, *Casting Nets: Grow Your Faith by Sharing Your Faith* (Huntington, IN: Our Sunday Visitor, 2015).

5. Pope Francis, "To Members of the Catholic Fraternity of Charismatic Covenant Communities and Fellowships" (address, Paul VI Audience Hall, Rome, Oct. 31, 2014).

6. Maria Faustina Kowalska, *Diary: Divine Mercy in My Soul* (Stockbridge, MA: Marian Press, 2005), 1397.

7. Also known as Abraham the Poor or Abraham the Simple.

8. Kowalska, *Diary,* 186–187.

9. Ibid, 1465.

10. Ibid., 1777.

11. Pope Francis, *Evangelii Gaudium,* 15.

12. Leonore Lang, *The Book of Heroes* (London: Longmans, Green, and Co., 1912), p. 331.

13. Pope Francis, *Evangelii Gaudium,* 153.

14. Ibid., 172.

15. Ibid., 114.

16. Fr. Reginald Marie Garrigou-Lagrange, O.P., *God, His Existence, and Nature,* vol. 2 (St. Louis: Herder, 1936), p. 412.

17. Pope Francis, *Evangelii Gaudium,* 24.

18. St. Benedict of Nursia, "Chapter 53: On the Reception of Guests," in *The Rule of St. Benedict.*

19. Pope Francis, *Evangelii Gaudium,* 63.

20. Pope Paul VI, Apostolic Exhortation, *Evangelii Nuntiandi* (Dec. 8, 1975), 21.

21. Pope Francis, *Evangelii Gaudium,* 150.

22. Ibid., 86.

23. Pope Paul VI, *Evangelii Nuntiandi,* 47.

24. Ibid., 28.

25. Pope Francis, *Evangelii Gaudium,* 160.

26. Ibid., 161.

27. Ibid., 127.

28. Ibid., 120.

29. Ibid., 173.

30. Pope Paul VI, Dogmatic Constitution on the Church, *Lumen Gentium* (Nov. 21, 1964), 40.

31. Pope Francis, *Evangelii Gaudium,* 21.

32. Ibid., 6.

33. Pope John Paul II, speech, July 16, 1989. FrassatiUSA website. https://frassatiusa.org/pollone-july-1989 (accessed June 30, 2017).

34. Pope Francis, *Evangelii Gaudium*, 272.

35. Ibid., 7.

36. Ibid., 10.

37. Pope Paul VI, *Evangelii Nuntiandi*, 76.

38. Pope Francis, Encyclical Letter, *Lumen Fidei* (Jun. 29, 2013), 34.

39. Pope Francis, Apostolic Exhortation, *Amoris Laetitia* (Mar. 19, 2016), 98.

40. Pope Francis, Bull of Indiction, *Misericordiae Vultus* (Apr. 11, 2015), 25.

41. Pope Francis, "To the Parish Priests of the Diocese of Rome" (address, Paul VI Audience Hall, Mar. 6, 2014). "Today we can think of the Church as a 'field hospital.' Excuse me but I repeat it, because this is how I see it, how I feel it is: a 'field hospital.' Wounds need to be treated, so many wounds! So many wounds! There are so many people who are wounded by material problems, by scandals, also in the Church…. People wounded by the world's illusions…. We priests must be there, close to these people. Mercy first means treating the wounds. When someone is wounded, he needs this immediately, not tests such as the level of cholesterol and one's glycemic index…. But there's a wound, treat the wound, and then we can look at the results of the tests. Then specialized treatments can be done, but first we need to treat the open wounds. I think this is what is most important at this time. And there are also hidden wounds, because there are people who distance themselves in order to avoid showing their wounds closer."

42. Pope Francis, *Misericordiae Vultus,* 10.

43. Pope Francis, *Evangelii Gaudium,* 3.

44. Pope Francis, *Misericordiae Vultus,* 9.

45. Ibid., 2.

46. Pope Francis, *Evangelii Gaudium,* 244.

47. Ibid., 239.

48. Pope Benedict XVI, Apostolic Letter, *Porta Fidei* (Oct. 11, 2011), 7.

49. Ibid., 10.

50. The orthodox correct position as defined by the first councils of the Church is that Jesus is one person who has two natures (human and divine). He is one hundred percent God and one hundred percent man (cf. *Catechism of the Catholic Church* [New York: Doubleday, 1994], 252, 468).

51. Pope Francis, *Evangelii Gaudium*, 86.

52. Ibid., 121.

53. Cf. Pope Benedict XVI, Encyclical Letter, *Spe Salvi* (Nov. 30, 2007), 4.

54. Pope Benedict XVI, *Spe Salvi,* 34.

55. Pope Francis, *Evangelii Gaudium,* 268.

56. Pope Paul VI, "To the Members of the Consilium de Laicis" (address, Rome, Oct. 2, 1974).

57. Pope Francis, *Evangelii Gaudium,* 179.

58. Pope Francis, Twitter post, Nov. 19, 2013, 7:19 a.m., http://twitter.com/Pontifex.

59. Pope St. John Paul II, Encyclical, *Redemptoris Missio* (Dec. 7, 1990), 90.

EVERY PARISH HAS A MISSION.
EVERY MISSION NEEDS A PLAN.

"The 7 Pillars have revitalized our parish and refocused us on our mission of evangelization.

What Casting Nets Ministries has developed is an absolute game-changer."

- Lois Locey
St. Magdalene Parish
Altamonte Springs, FL

In our evangelization primer, *Casting Nets: Grow Your Faith by Sharing Your Faith*, we presented the 7 Pillars of Effective Evangelization©, which we have identified as the core principles for sharing the Gospel and making disciples.

These same 7 Pillars can be applied to Catholic Parishes, Schools, apostolates, and ministry groups, since the fundamental reason they exist is to evangelize and make Christ known.

To that end, our team of evangelists and pastoral experts have developed **The 7 Pillars Pastoral Plan©**, a revolutionary pastoral planning process that helps parishes, schools, and apostolates:

Assess and evaluate their pastoral situation and mission effectiveness
Identify key strengths and areas of weakness
Discern needs, resources, and opportunities
Develop a practical plan of action that implements the 7 Pillars
Train and equip your members in the fundamentals of evangelization
Foster a culture of missionary discipleship and stewardship

Let us help you create a culture of missionary discipleship & evangelization in your parish! Contact us for a free consultation today! (800)217-5710

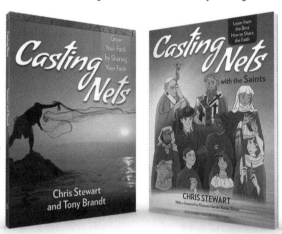